ARCHITECTURE 03

GW00500232

ARCHITECTURE 03

THE RIBA AWARDS

EDITED BY TONY CHAPMAN

RIBA ⌗

MERRELL
LONDON · NEW YORK

First published 2003 by Merrell Publishers Limited

Head office: 42 Southwark Street, London SE1 1UN
Telephone +44 (0)20 7403 2047
E-mail mail@merrellpublishers.com

New York office: 49 West 24th Street, New York, NY 10010
Telephone +1 212 929 8344
E-mail info@merrellpublishersusa.com

www.merrellpublishers.com

PUBLISHER Hugh Merrell
US DIRECTOR Joan Brookbank
EDITORIAL DIRECTOR Julian Honer
MANAGING EDITOR Anthea Snow
EDITOR Sam Wythe
DESIGN MANAGER Kate Ward
PRODUCTION MANAGER Michelle Draycott
SALES AND MARKETING DIRECTOR Emilie Amos
SALES AND MARKETING EXECUTIVE Emily Sanders

Text copyright © 2003 Royal Institute of British Architects
Photographs copyright © the photographers and architects; see photo credits for details
Design and layout copyright © 2003 Merrell Publishers Limited

All rights reserved. No part of this publication may be reproduced, stored in a retrieval system or
transmitted, in any form or by any means, electronic, mechanical, photocopying, recording or otherwise,
without the prior permission in writing from the publisher.

British Library Cataloguing-in-Publication Data:
Chapman, Tony, 1953–
Architecture 03 : the RIBA awards
1.Architecture – Awards – Great Britain 2.Architecture – Europe – 21st century
I.Title II.Royal Institute of British Architects
720.9′4′09051
ISBN 1 85894 244 6

Produced by Merrell Publishers
Designed by Claudia Schenk, edited by Tom Neville
Printed and bound in Great Britain by TFW Printers, London

CONTENTS

JUDGING THE STIRLING PRIZE 2003

Eight years on and the Stirling Prize has truly arrived. These days I can't take a cab or buy a paper without getting my ear bent about what should win this year. Architecture is no longer just the stuff of dinner-party conversations in Clerkenwell and Edinburgh; they're talking about it in greasy spoons in Todmorden and Penge. And that's largely down to Stirling and Channel 4. People have woken up to the fact that architecture is important, and not before time: they've been living, working and playing in it all their lives. They're becoming more discriminating, too, not only about the buildings in which they live and work, but also about other people's, the buildings that they brush up against in their daily lives. The Stirling Prize is unashamedly aspirational. If *Changing Rooms* is the *Sun* and *Mirror* of design on television, *Grand Designs* the *Daily Mail*, then Channel 4's coverage of the Stirling Prize in *Building of the Year* is the *Guardian* and *Telegraph*. The programme is wall-to-wall architecture, stiff with architects and architecture critics. It's the only programme that makes the audience swallow the pill uncoated – and they appear to be getting a taste for the treatment. Nor is the programme ghettoized on cable; it's there on terrestrial at peak time, 8 pm on a Sunday evening. In my day – before I became an architectural bureaucrat I used to make TV programmes – you were lucky to get architecture on the box at all and only then by mentioning Prince Charles – even if critically – every five minutes. Channel 4's programme addresses an intelligent lay audience; it does not, as some architects would have it, indulge in the archi-speak many in the profession use for communication. Nor does it allow the buildings to speak for themselves, but then not all buildings are sufficiently articulate. As well as using the camera to explore the buildings in much the same way as the human eye does, Waldemar Januszczak speaks for and occasionally against them. Architecture today is big enough to take it. And it can safely be assumed that to get on the Stirling shortlist a building must be pretty good.

This year there are six of them. For the first time there is nothing outside the UK, but there is still a good geographic spread from Plymouth to the Isle of Tiree in the Hebrides, with indubitably an over-representation of four buildings in Greater London. This is less surprising when you remember that 40 per cent of the UK's architects are based in the south east. The region is the major economic generator and buildings get built where people need and can afford them. The RIBA Stirling Prize in association with *The Architects' Journal* is the culmination of the most rigorous judging process in architecture. The winner, along with the other five shortlisted buildings, will have been judged by three or four separate juries, each comprising architects and non-architects. Entered in the first quarter of the year, they will have been pulled apart by a regional panel (and visited if there is any doubt as to whether they should progress further); visited by a jury including an architect from the region, one from elsewhere and a 'lay' juror – engineer, client, contractor, journalist, etc. In April a meeting at the RIBA brings together the Awards Group (the scheme's advisory panel) and the chairs of the 14 regional juries. Nancy Mills, who has been administering the awards for 25 years with a patience bordering on the saintly, has the unenviable job of mounting all the entries recommended for awards in one room, and all those not recommended next door. A long day begins with the group sifting through these, a process that produces a number of challenges to the regional jury chairs: the why-nots. A more detailed study of the recommendations leads to a small collection of whys. The jury chair now has a half-hour slot to justify his or her jury's thinking. If there is still disagreement when the time is up, and the next chair is knocking at the door, members have to pay another, what could be a third, visit. And, still true to the principle that no project is rejected by people who haven't seen it, they have the final say. The Awards Group reconvenes a few days later, having had time to mull over what they have heard and seen (or already know personally). The 60 to 70 now-confirmed awards announced at a posh dinner in June, are now reduced to a dozen or so: the Stirling midlist.

Awards are not a test of the prose style used by the architects in their entries, but slap-dash descriptions (or over-wrought over-long ones) do not help; nor is this a photographic competition, but fuzzy images certainly don't help either. And many buildings on the midlist do select themselves: excellence will rise to the surface – as one previous juror pontificated after several pints of the stuff in Dublin – like the smooth cream head on a glass of Guinness. If in doubt, there are pages upon pages of criteria available to the judges at every stage, doubtless learned by rote by each and every one of them. But, less tangibly, there is a sense of what it takes to make up a good midlist and therefore shortlist. No, there are no geographical, sexual or racial quotas (some would argue that there should be); there is nothing to say that there should be a range of projects by size of budget; nor by age and experience of architects; certainly not by style. But all these considerations are there hovering at the back of the collective consciousness; if a good scheme comes up that does tick one or more of these boxes, it will be seriously discussed.

At that April meeting lists are also drawn up for the special awards: Client of the Year, the Stephen Lawrence Prize for the best scheme under £350,000, The Architects' Journal First Building; as well as awards for conservation, access and sustainability. These are judged by members of the Awards Group and relevant experts (and sponsors): the Crown Estate, the ADAPT Trust, and so on. Yet more visits. You can see why some clients appear distinctly jaded as they show yet another jury round their pride but diminishing source of joy, with still no guarantee of a result.

But those of us involved in the judging love it. The architects in particular: they're usually too busy to get round to seeing what the opposition is up to. Maybe it's the continuing professional development architects are obliged to undertake, but architects are perpetual students, ever willing to learn, to debate with their peers, to find inspiration in the work of others. All in all, they're a remarkably generous bunch too. For me, and I suspect for the other non-architects, seeing buildings in the company of architects is a real privilege. Already this year I've seen Santiago de Compostela Cathedral through the eyes of an architectural historian, Giles Worsley – it wasn't on this year's list but it was handy for David Chipperfield's house – and I've watched Eric Parry sketch out an early idea for a competition entry, on a train from Cornwall. These are the bonuses. In between I'm there to drive or make sure trains and planes aren't missed and that Nancy's precise schedules are stuck to; to film the buildings to share with members of the group who weren't able to be on that particular trip and to show at the Stirling dinner, should the subject prove to be a winner; and to find that my own lay views are taken surprisingly seriously – I've picked up quite a bit in eight years; after all, I could have been qualified in less time. This year there's a further complication. We want the best architects on the Awards Group and the best architects tend to produce the best buildings. That means designing and building a series of Chinese walls worthy of an award themselves. Any members of the group with a scheme up for consideration have, of course, to absent themselves from any visit or discussion of their building or its rivals. All summer people are hopping on and off buses and ducking in and out of rooms, killing time until it's safe for them to return. Three of them, including the chair of the group, are missing from the lunch at the RIBA where we agree the final shortlist of six.

Now it's all down to the final judging, by yet another jury. Led by RIBA President George Ferguson, the jury comprises last year's winner (and the year before's), Chris Wilkinson; Isabel Allen, editor of *The Architects' Journal*, our main sponsor; twice Booker-shortlisted novelist Julian Barnes; and Justine Frischmann, who did six of the seven years it takes to become an architect before giving it all up to sing with Elastica and now co-presents BBC TV's architecture programme *Dream Spaces*. The visits take place over four days in September, two of which are spent getting on and off Tiree. Each day there is only one flight in and one flight out – and that takes off half an hour after landing, doing Queen's Award-meriting service to the island's hotel industry. It is a bit like being on *Big Brother*-meets-*Fantasy-Island*-meets-*Survivor*. marooned on an island with no escape. Tiree is best known for its regular appearances on the shipping forecast. Now we know why: having spent a couple of hours being shown round (along?) Sutherland Hussey's slender building by the hugely enthusiastic client, Brian Milne, the weather closes in and we're threatened with three days on the island – no Sabbath flights here. In the end – and after a long night's bonding over dinner and in the bar afterwards – the wind abates, the cloud lifts and we get away, leaving Brian muttering dark threats about slashing the tyres of the local councillor who dared to poke mild fun at the shelter in the *Scottish Daily Mail* for not providing comfy seats or a decent cup of coffee. They take their architecture seriously in these parts.

Day three sees us in a bus and on our way to Plymouth to look at TR2, which turns out to be not a vintage car but Ian Ritchie's Plymouth Theatre Royal 2 – their production centre and rehearsal rooms. The bronze-mesh pods gleam and the granite beach, heaved out of an abandoned quarry across the way, sparkles in the Indian-summer sun, putting us all in a good mood. This is a place done on a spectacular scale: assembly areas big enough to build whole sets upright and rehearsal spaces bigger than the stages back at the city-centre theatre. C4 love it too for the people-sized steel TR2 by the main entrance where they get the judges to look as if they're auditioning for a 1960s album cover, wrapping themselves round the characters.

The final day and a magical mystery tour round the capital, starting in Beddington near Sutton. BedZED is a genuinely eco-friendly housing scheme, topped off with colourful Mickey Mouse-ear-shaped chimney cowls. The judges are shown round by an enthusiastic resident, while the architect Bill Dunster cowers nervously in his on-site office – the rules don't permit architects to give the judges the tour. Everyone admires its green credentials – for once the brave eco-words are translated into action – not all like its rough and ready aesthetic – you have to be there to appreciate it. George Ferguson for one is a keen convert and a great admirer of the architect's bloody-mindedness.

Herzog & de Meuron's Laban, our next stop, suffers from front-runner-itis. It's William Hill's favourite and that of many architects too, but all our judges are seeing it for the first time, in the company of Anthony Bowne. Since the midlist visit, he has taken over as director from Dr Marion North, whose lifetime project this is. There are two more changes: the dramatic grass-terraced landscaping is nearing completion and the place is alive with beautiful dancers who grace the corridors as elegantly as they do the studios. Even the porters here like to pose.

The sun is shining on Eric Parry's 30 Finsbury Square. The building takes up half of one side of the square and shows up everything else on view. The strong light models the façade, giving it depth, making it look like a building within a building. Justine in particular is just as enthusiastic about the cool interiors. None of us has the remotest idea what the money men and women get up to in here, but they seem perfectly happy, so the spaces are clearly working.

Finally – an hour late by now – we make it to Foster's Great Court at the British Museum. All our tiredness is forgotten as we enter this magnificent space and our spirits soar. Great buildings repeat this trick, no matter how often you see them. On a first visit you spend all your time looking up at the brilliant roof but there is so much more to discover above and below ground. Ken Stannard is keen to show us how the court has made sense of a previously nonsensical building. He even gets us up on the roof – on the last judging trip they couldn't find the key – and we gain a new perspective on the scheme by peering through the lip of the glass roof. Those of us who have worked here in the past can scarcely recognize the old museum.

It's a fitting end to four exciting days of visits. Now the judges have four weeks to reflect in tranquillity on what they have seen, before meeting up at Explore @ Bristol, to choose this year's winner. Which is …

THE STIRLING PRIZE

THE STIRLING PRIZE 2003

IN ASSOCIATION WITH THE ARCHITECTS' JOURNAL

The RIBA Stirling Prize, now in its eighth year, is for the third year sponsored by *The Architects' Journal*. It is awarded to the architects of the building thought to be the most significant of the year for the evolution of architecture and the built environment. It is the UK's richest and most prestigious architectural prize. The winners receive a cheque for £20,000 and a trophy, which they hold for one year.

The prize is named after the architect Sir James Stirling (1926–92), one of the most important British architects of his generation and a progressive thinker and designer throughout his career. He is best known for his Leicester University Engineering Building (1959–63), the Staatsgalerie in Stuttgart (1977–84) and his posthumous Number One Poultry building in London. His former partner Michael Wilford won the 1997 Stirling Prize for the jointly designed Stuttgart Music School, and this year won an RIBA Award for the History Museum which completed Stirling's masterplan for the Stuttgart Staatsgalerie complex.

The winner of the 2003 RIBA Stirling Prize in association with *The Architects' Journal* was

LABAN, DEPTFORD, LONDON SE8, BY HERZOG & DE MEURON

LABAN
.DEPTFORD, LONDON SE8 .HERZOG & DE MEURON

Laban has given Deptford a significant and beautiful new landmark. The building is a singular and simple container with a double-skinned wall. This is constructed of a delicate external membrane of coloured polycarbonate concealing a utilitarian and economical inner layer of insulation and translucent glass panels. At carefully considered moments, the inner and outer worlds are more immediately connected by ambiguously scaled, framed transparent panels. This compositional device is cleverly mirrored in the plan form, punctuated by spaces of various heights and shape related to their function. The rectangular plan is warped by the tension of the gentle curve that both welcomes the visitor and responds to the verticality of the nearby St Paul's Church Deptford.

The dance studios are pressed up against the external envelope and use the exquisite coloured translucency of the walls to separate the plane of the timber floors from the massive ribbed-concrete soffits. The labyrinthine quality of the internal circulation is dramatized by the high chroma of the wall paint, dark-toned interiors, lightwells and, most dramatically, the sculptural gloss black-painted spiral stairs, one at the front, the other at the rear. The creative world of dance is matched by that of art and architecture.

Laban will do for dance what Tate Modern has done for art, announces a screen inside the entrance to this less-grandiloquent but equally eloquent building by the Swiss pair. And it is true: there is a buzz about the place from the moment you step inside the translucent polychromatic polycarbonate screen. The space ramps up towards studios and theatres or down towards the café and treatment centres. All the activities of the dance centre are intermixed and distributed on two levels, promoting communication throughout this complex building. The basic form is a rectangular box, but it is subverted with a few breathtaking moves, such as that caved-in façade, which leads the eye out towards the church but also marks the entrance. Inside, circulation takes the form of an H around the main theatre and is defined by the two lightwells (a third was sadly lost to economies). Each of the eleven studios has a subtly different size, height, form and colour.

CLIENT LABAN
STRUCTURAL ENGINEER WHITBYBIRD
SERVICES ENGINEER WHITBYBIRD
THEATRE CONSULTANT CARR & ANGIER
ACOUSTICS CONSULTANT ARUP ACOUSTICS
LANDSCAPE ARCHITECT VOGT
LANDSCHAFTARCHITEKTEN, ZURICH
QS DAVIS LANGDON & EVEREST
CONTRACTOR BALLAST CONSTRUCTION
COST £14.4 MILLION
PHOTOGRAPHERS MERLIN HENDY /
MARTYN ROSE, PAGES 16–17, 19, 21
(BOTTOM); MERLIN HENDY, PAGE 21
(TOP); DENNIS GILBERT – VIEW, PAGE
20; WILL PRYCE, PAGE 21 (CENTRE)

This is a building whose architectural ambition and ideas are realized at the highest level. Throughout, the selection and detailing of materials provides a beautiful luminance. The quality of light – both from the inside out and the outside in – is exceptionally beautiful for occupants, visitors and neighbours. The transparent polycarbonate panels were devised in collaboration with the artist Michael Craig-Martin. Mounted in front of the glass, they serve as a protective sun shield and improve the building's energy efficiency – as well as being objects of beauty in their own right.

The building is inventive in the way its form reveals the choreography of movement. The public circulation spaces are full of wit in the curving handrail, which counters the hard line of the dance-studio bar. This is a project in which the design vision is carried through from the first ideas to its completed detail. The extent of innovation in the project is apparent throughout but never shouted. It is a graceful building, generous in its relationship to its context: its reference to St Paul's Church is geometrically precise, while it is calmly haphazard alongside the meandering of Deptford Creek.

The judges thought this to be an extraordinarily fine building, one that raises the expectations of architecture in its engagement both with art forms and with the local context; it makes a major contribution to the artistic life of the community while acting as a catalyst to the regeneration of the whole area.

Julian Barnes summed up the feelings of the Stirling jury: 'It hits you straight between the eyes as soon as you get there. It has the same movement, youth, agility, pzzaz, front to it that its students have – it's very seductive. The immediate reaction of everyone in the bus as we arrived was to go "Wow".'

ALSO SHORTLISTED FOR THE ADAPT TRUST ACCESS AWARD; DR MARION NORTH SHORTLISTED FOR RIBA CLIENT OF THE YEAR

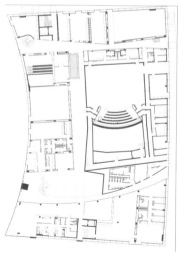

GROUND-FLOOR PLAN

BEDZED
.WALLINGTON .BILL DUNSTER ARCHITECTS

BedZED is a 21st-century take on the English Garden City. It is the first large-scale 'carbon-neutral' community in the United Kingdom, helping its residents to cut carbon emissions from personal transport, from that involved in bringing their food to the door, as well as from running their homes. As such it is exemplary sustainable-housing design. Predicted energy savings are in the region of 60 per cent. Grey and black water are processed on site. It employs a whole range of sustainable technologies. To achieve this in a one-off experimental house would have been good going; to do it in a publicly funded mixed-tenure housing scheme is quite astonishing.

Even before visiting the place expectations are set high, accompanied by a nagging doubt that one might be assaulted by hairshirt worthiness. However, this doubt is swept away by the sheer exuberance of the place. The multi-coloured wind cowls may be reminiscent of Mickey Mouse, but this is no Mickey Mouse architecture: it is serious stuff. What is so refreshing is that the innovations in sustainable design are accompanied by, or have led to, innovations in spatial design. The flats and houses are a delight to be in, full of light and incident. The use of the sunspaces, generally double-height glazed areas, as environmental buffers, makes possible a whole range of variations in the way the accommodation is occupied throughout the year.

The high density of the scheme does not lead to claustrophobia, mainly because of the clever manipulation in section that gives a patch of private external space to each unit. Best of all are the sky gardens, reached over bridges, providing a sense of release and expansion.

BedZED jolts one into revising the architectural value system, raising consciousness of a much wider set of issues than the niceties of a detail. On the day of the judges' visit the place was swarming with school children learning exactly how these issues impact on their daily lives. But BedZED is more than a demonstration project – that suggests it would remain as a one-off to be admired in the corner. What is clear is that the lessons learnt and

CLIENT DICKON ROBINSON, THE PEABODY TRUST
STRUCTURAL ENGINEER ELLIS AND MOORE
SERVICES ENGINEER ARUP
ENVIRONMENTAL CONSULTANT BIOREGIONAL DEVELOPMENT
CONTRACTOR GARDINER & THEOBALD CONSTRUCTION MANAGEMENT
COST £15 MILLION
PHOTOGRAPHER ZEDFACTORY.COM

techniques employed can and should be applied across a wide range of future housing schemes, both public and private. Few schemes built in the United Kingdom over the last few years can be said to have genuinely moved on architectural knowledge and culture. BedZED is one that has.

Some 95 per cent of the structural steel was sourced within an average 56-kilometre radius of the site, mostly from Brighton station, which was being refurbished at the time. None of the steel was melted down; it was simply employed as found, so that evidence of its original use can be seen in the houses. The architects even stopped the contractors grinding the steel down to make it appear new. Bill Dunster reckons most workaday buildings could use recycled steel in this way, though even he agrees the British Museum roof might prove an exception.

The aim at BedZED is not just to make housing and workspaces that are sustainable, but also to create a new architectural language. This vision is reflected in all aspects of the design and is carried through with hi-tech and low-tech solutions, such as the provision of surplus electricity to charge electric-powered bikes, a system of shared car use and smart-card technology. But BedZED is not preachy. Those school children were thoroughly enjoying their lesson but they seemed to be utterly unaware that that was what it was. They were simply having fun.

George Ferguson summarized on behalf of the Stirling judges: 'BedZED is doing the trick: it is opening people's eyes to what is possible, to the necessity not to compromise, and that I really admire. Too often as architects we are driven to compromise and here we've got a bloody-mindedness that I would encourage, not in an arrogant way but in a mission-driven way, from an architect who really does believe that we are threatened if we don't improve on the performance of buildings.'

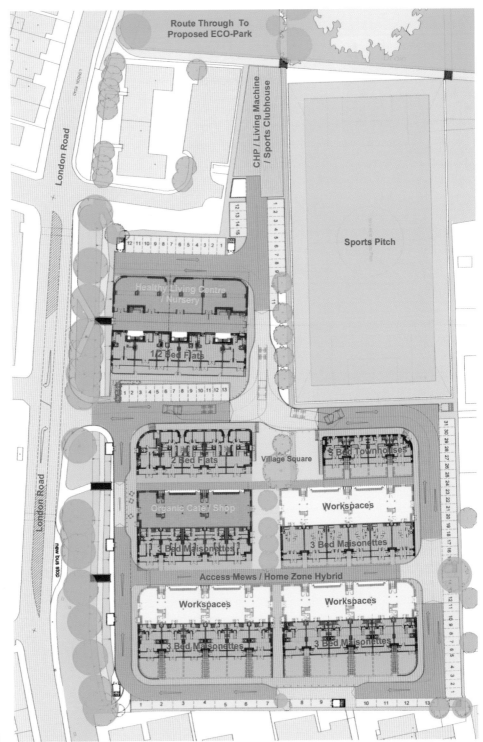

Route Through To
Proposed ECO-Park

London Road

CHP / Living Machine
/ Sports Clubhouse

Sports Pitch

Healthy Living Centre
/ Nursery

1/2 Bed Flats

2 Bed Flats

Village Square

3 Bed Townhouses

Organic Cafe / Shop

Workspaces

3 Bed Maisonettes

3 Bed Maisonettes

Access Mews / Home Zone Hybrid

Workspaces

Workspaces

3 Bed Maisonettes

3 Bed Maisonettes

London Road

new bus stop

SITE PLAN

30 FINSBURY SQUARE
.LONDON EC2 .ERIC PARRY ARCHITECTS

30 Finsbury Square is a very modern building in a highly traditional setting that works supremely well for its users. Unlike any speculative commercial office building completed in and around the City of London in recent years, it owes its external appearance and internal characteristics to the architect's bold decision to exploit the possibilities of load-bearing stone as the crucial material and structural element in the design.

Dictated by the local planning authority's conservation policy, the use of stone has resulted in a deep screen on the front façade, with the placement of piers representing load 'hot spots'. There is nothing arbitrary about the final result, which gives significant column-free space for the office interiors. The internal atrium is as dramatic as it is unexpected, given the low-key nature of the entrance itself; light enters the interiors, not least the basement space, in a variety of ways. The way the façade changes from the front to the rear elevation gives an indication of the economy of thinking (as well as economy of construction) that informs this project and that has offered a new proposition about the use of 'traditional' materials in a market dominated by steel, glass and aluminium.

The idea for the building was born out of an idea for reworking Finsbury Square. The most difficult part of the design was to persuade the public – through the planning process – that a new building could be as good as a locally listed building that had to be demolished; so it was about conservation of the square for the future. The architects had also to contend with a prescriptive design guide for the square; this prefers the use of Portland stone, a vertical emphasis and a given building height. A very special solution was then found to all these problems and parameters, resulting in a stunning office environment and a building that makes an important contribution to the square. Offices make up 80 per cent of the fabric of the City of London, yet they have always been built pragmatically in as short a time and as cheaply as possible. Façades have tended to be treated like bathroom tiling. The brilliance of this scheme is in the inversion of that thinking by creating a load-bearing façade and separating it from the glazed interior.

CLIENT JONES LANG LASALLE
STRUCTURAL ENGINEER WHITBYBIRD
SERVICES ENGINEER HILSON MORAN
PARTNERSHIP
QS GARDINER & THEOBALD
CONTRACTOR HBG CONSTRUCTION
COST £26 MILLION
PHOTOGRAPHER HÉLÈNE BINET

The project, then, represents a marriage between the urban archetype of the London square and the office building, a hybrid that has produced a novel technical solution. These ground-breaking offices, though expressed as a stone building, have a heart of steel. They are constructed with beautifully made solid Portland stone load-bearing columns and stone-clad transfer beams at every floor level. A 15-metre clear span links the façade back to a frame construction around the atrium and core. The span helps to satisfy the needs of the City for large floorplates. What is unique about the design of the façade is the way it allows the masonry to be stacked, while allowing for movement behind it. This means that every beam has to be different. The atrium has four simple steel columns, but in order to allow for a full-width entrance sequence, these are braced by a steel truss at first-floor level. The detailing throughout is exquisite and the fit-out, by different designers, is for once complementary.

On the rear, north side, where the context is street not square, the building has a similar patterning to that of the southern façade, but here the windows are brought out to the face between columns and beams, reflecting the reduced heat-gain load for this façade. Here the masonry is not load-bearing but instead takes the form of a rainscreen hung on a simple steel frame.

For the Stirling judges, Chris Wilkinson concluded: 'It has a lightness of touch and quality of detail that raises the level of architecture. It is an architect's building but, from the outside, I think everyone could appreciate its qualities. Inside, it's very simple, flexible office space

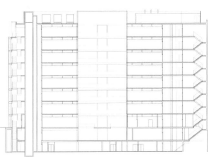

SECTION

GREAT COURT AT THE BRITISH MUSEUM
.LONDON WC1 .FOSTER & PARTNERS

The Great Court is an exceptional project in that it realizes the potential of the British Museum. It is difficult to think of another British public building that has been so completely transformed in terms of both perception and use through the introduction of such a grand yet simple concept.

The strength of the project lies in the clarity of the central idea: turning the building outside in, converting a forgotten courtyard into the primary space that creates a public focus and links galleries previously only accessible on a linear, prescribed route. The Great Court make possible a different experience of galleries, vertically and horizontally, allowing visitors to enjoy their own selection of exhibits, free from the usual chronological sequence. Smirke's magnificent Reading Room, previously hidden and inaccessible, is now placed at the heart of the museum, visible from various levels.

While the glazed roof and central stone addition to the Reading Room are the most obvious parts of the project, much of the £100 million scheme involves reworking the bowels of the museum to provide excellent lecture and education spaces, again easily accessed from the public concourse and enriching the experience of the place. The quality of the design and construction, however, also lies in the detail, creating a consistent, controlled language that engages with the original building. Perhaps the greatest success of the Great Court is that it has transformed the perceived character of the British Museum from that of a dry institution to an informal forum, offering food, drink and sheer space to enjoy – a real *tour de force*.

Originally built as an open garden, the court was soon filled by the Reading Room and later by other ancillary storage structures. The departure of the British Library to Euston allowed the creation of a generous circulation space at the heart of the museum. The client deserves recognition for conceiving the principle of a grand roof over the court at the competition stage.

At this stage, the architects specified a canopy of inflated ETFE pillows, because of their thermal characteristics and capacity to block ultra-violet

CLIENT THE BRITISH MUSEUM
HISTORIC BUILDING ADVISORS GILES QUARME ASSOCIATES / CAROE & PARTNERS / IAN BRISTOW
STRUCTURAL ENGINEER BURO HAPPOLD
SERVICES ENGINEER BURO HAPPOLD
QS NORTHCROFT NICHOLSON
CONTRACTOR MACE LTD
COST £100 MILLION
PHOTOGRAPHER NIGEL YOUNG

radiation. But another apparent advantage turned out to be quite the opposite: it was so light that it needed an ugly and inappropriately heavy steel structure to hold it down. Instead Waagner Biro, the Viennese firm that built the Reichstag's cupola, came up with a design for a roof that is supported only at its edges and at the centre, where a ring of steel columns is hidden behind the new stone façade of the Reading Room. The roof sections were prefabricated off-site and lowered into position using lasers to align them. When the roof was de-propped, the structure dropped 150 millimetres and spread 90 millimetres like a sheet of silk. It behaved exactly as predicted by the engineers – complex geometry translated into reality.

On walking through the new portico the impression is dramatic, amplified by the gloom of the previous spaces. The design, detailing and construction of the glazed canopy creates a stunning effect, especially on a sunny day when the shadow play from the roof structure adds greatly to the character of the space. The roof is magnificent. Two new sweeping staircases flanking the Reading Room greet the visitor approaching from the main entrance and their inviting appearance successfully draws people to the temporary exhibition gallery and the restaurant on the upper levels, while also providing powerful elevated views down into the court. The Great Court is a welcome and powerful addition to the rich cultural experiences of London.

George Ferguson spoke for the rest of the Stirling judges when he said: 'I think it is one of the supreme achievements of the new millennium and will be seen as such in a hundred years time. It has opened our eyes to the interior of the British Museum, it has made it a public place; it is of supreme quality. Norman, Spencer de Grey and Buro Happold have taken the brief and added a bit of magic. This is a very good example of a design team all working together to produce a marriage of architecture and engineering.'

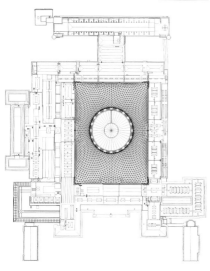

ROOF-LEVEL PLAN

and let thy feet
millenniums hence
be set in midst of knowledge

PLYMOUTH THEATRE ROYAL PRODUCTION CENTRE .PLYMOUTH .IAN RITCHIE ARCHITECTS

Driving out of Plymouth along the coast, beyond the rows of houses is a scraggy area of tin sheds and culs-de-sac. Here, on the edge of a small harbour, among the abattoirs and call-centres, a new building has been designed for the Theatre Royal. The site has all the grimy glamour of a half-derelict industrial zone. This is a backstage building in a backstage place.

The production centre is the result of a truly collaborative relationship between architect and client. The architect was involved in the choice of site, then involved the client by asking for a wish-list of requirements for the building. A big shed was always going to be the answer, given the client's stated need for tall production bays, assembly, wardrobe, prop-making and rehearsal facilities for the city-centre based Theatre Royal. Ian Ritchie clearly relished the brief and location. He has made a robust factory building on the edge of the water. The site is part land-fill, part land-art. The ground at the edge of the water is reclaimed from the harbour and it forms a raised storm barrier. Made from broken stone, it slopes in a long even line down to the sea. The building is placed on this pulverized rock podium, giving the scheme an almost zen-like appearance.

The building is organized into three clear parts: a large shed for assembling stage sets; a long bar of workshops relating to the manufacture of sets; and a series of independent rooms for rehearsal. The three kinds of elements are clearly articulated and different cladding materials signify each type. The shed is covered in opalescent glass to allow even illumination of the interior, the workshops are wrapped in almost matching standing-seam zinc, and the rehearsal rooms are kitted out in a fabulous quilted anorak of phosphor-bronze mesh. The beauty of this assembly is that the grey, bronze and brown of the building are haunted by a ghostly green that seems hidden within every material. It is like a muted bass line holding the various materials together.

The interior of the building is very matter of fact. Simple materials and clear graphics signify the working nature of the place. The industrial elements are

CLIENT PLYMOUTH THEATRE ROYAL
STRUCTURAL ENGINEER ARUP
SERVICES ENGINEER ARUP
QS DAVIS LANGDON & EVEREST
CONTRACTOR BLUESTONE
COST £5.8 MILLION
PHOTOGRAPHER JOCELYNE VAN DEN BOSSCHE

organized as a simple functional nave with set assembly, workshops, dressing, costume, offices and rest rooms linked along a 'straight as a die' glazed route stretching from reception to service entrance. The route connects user and visitor to all the activities, enjoying the southward estuary view and sunlit big sky. Assembly and production is noisy and dusty so the opportunity has been seen to place the rehearsal spaces as sealed soap bubbles. This transforms the big-shed idea into a sort of theatrical hive. The Crittall windows to the rehearsal spaces often afford surprising views of passing shipping. This main construction workshop is double-height, allowing sufficient headroom for complete sets to be constructed and assembled. So rare is this facility that the theatre is able to undertake work for outside companies, including the Royal Opera, helping the new centre to pay for itself. The rehearsal rooms sit on the rock-armour platform like objects of contemplation. They are like nothing else – half chainmail coat, half puffa-jacket. By lifting them off the ground with a tilted ring of glass, they are made to float. This is pure architectural drama. Ritchie plays with our perception of weight, mass and materials.

It is fortunate that the clients found the right architect for this programme and place. Ian Ritchie's muted, almost bitter, palate has conjured a strange, awkward beauty from a barren stretch of shore. This is a building that is beautifully shaped around its users. Actors and directors have praised it as an inspiring place in which to work.

Speaking for the Stirling judges, Isabel Allen summed it up: 'I love it. The drama of the building is saved for the outside, which is a very respectful thing; it's not detracting from the craft but it gives something back to Plymouth. You walk into the building and it's got a slightly rough-and-ready feel. What's wonderful is that it's made this kind of monumentality out of this backstage craft; it hasn't tried to be anything else.'

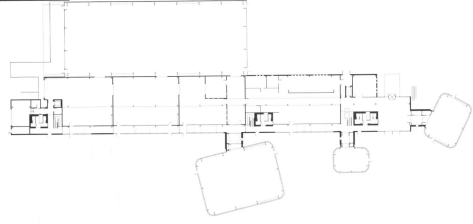

GROUND-FLOOR PLAN

TIREE SHELTER — AN TURAS .TIREE .SUTHERLAND HUSSEY ARCHITECTS WITH JAKE HARVEY, DONALD URQUHART, GLEN ONWIN, SANDRA KENNEDY

An Turas is Gaelic for journey; here the journey involves all the senses. Entering the shelter, the wind is deadened, human voices are heightened but change as you walk its length, between the hard narrow white walls (almost blinding in sudden sunshine), into the timber-slatted covered bridge, finally emerging into the glass and steel belvedere that frames a view of a white dot of a building on the far shore. This is architecture and art made inseparable.

Tiree seems to float off the Scottish mainland, tied by the umbilical cord of its airport and pierheads. The nearby pier, a modern affair of brutish concrete with an array of sheds, pens, offices and scattered houses, acts as the arrival and departure point by sea but does not begin to hint at the island's delightful natural and man-made landscape.

Although tiny, this collaborative project between architects, artists and an engineer reflects many of the monumental qualities of the place – the big sky and horizon, the white beach, the monochrome black houses dotted over the land – all distilled as a line in the landscape. It is both artwork and viewing platform. Two parallel walls in white render cut through a sloping hillside. They continue as two black timber walls joined by timber roof and floor to form a covered bridge across a rocky outcrop. The narrow passageway culminates in a glass box that crashes through a traditional dry-stone wall. Looking down the passageway from its entrance, you see a framed view across a sea bay of a perfectly ordinary stretch of flat, treeless, brightly lit Tiree, containing a perfectly ordinary house. But as you approach and arrive at the glass box, the picture opens up and is made magical by the surrounding sky, foreshore and sea. The new viewing platform is a kind of a palliative to the chaos of impressions that greets the visitor at this pierhead. Essentially it is a telescope that, once entered, frames an exquisite fragment of sky, house, foreshore, beach and water. In a landscape where all is battened down to survive the gales, the pavilion elevates the soul, providing an appropriately calm oasis amid the ugliness of contemporary life.

CLIENT TIREE ARTS ENTERPRISE
STRUCTURAL ENGINEER DAVID NARRO ENGINEERS
CONTRACTOR INSCAPE JOINERY
COST £95,000
PHOTOGRAPHERS DONALD URQUHART; EXCEPT PAGE 41, TOP, COLIN HUSSEY

A very moving piece of architectural sculpture has been created out of the mundane requirement for a tiny shelter from the wind. This is both the sunniest and the windiest place in the UK. So although this is a low-level linear structure, strength was essential. And because the rendered walls are unroofed, they need to be self-supporting to withstand regular 70-mile-an-hour winds. The glass box had to be made up on the mainland and was transported and craned into position, an expensive and even hazardous procedure necessitated by a lack of skilled labour on the island.

The shelter is not treated reverentially, either by people or its surroundings. One islander said, yes it frames the view but the view was fine without it; others refer to it as two walls and a telephone box with no phone; and the owners of the bungalow framed by the landward view are not best pleased at losing part of their own seaward view. It is squeezed between rusting cattle pens and a new Calmac ferry terminal building, which Charlie Hussey has dubbed 'the Pizza Hut'. A letter in the local paper encouraged people to graffiti their comments on the shelter's white walls. Yet *An Turas* remains pristine, the islanders are coming to respect, even to love it, and they are excited by the attention that it and their island have received. In many ways, it sums up the place: a low white building, crouched against the wind, a thing of mystery and strange beauty.

Justine Frischmann summed up the views of the Stirling judges: 'It feels like a very special space to me; almost like walking into a church, it's a spiritual experience. This is the most artistic side of architecture; it really lifts your spirits and that's what great art or architecture should do. It's beyond function.'

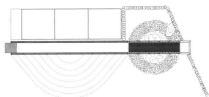

PLAN

SPECIAL AWARDS

ADAPT TRUST ACCESS AWARD

The ADAPT Trust Access Award is given to the architects of an arts or heritage building that goes way beyond the demands of building regulations and provides access for people of all abilities by considering their needs from the outset of a project, not bolting on solutions as an afterthought.

The first winner in 2001 was the Royal Academy of Dramatic Arts (RADA) in London, and last year's was Dance Base, Edinburgh.

The ADAPT Trust was set up in 1989 following a report by Lord Attenborough on access to arts buildings. It carries out audits on existing buildings and advises on new ones, bearing in mind not just the obvious needs of wheelchair users, but also those of people with hearing difficulties and visual impairment, whose problems in using buildings can be just as great. It is not just a matter of ramps and signs, it is about the whole way spaces relate in buildings, about lateral as well as vertical movement and about the acoustic behaviour of surfaces. It is also about getting value for money by doing the right things at the right time, and not having to resort to costly add-ons.

The 2003 shortlist was
HAMPSTEAD THEATRE, LONDON NW3, BY BENNETTS ASSOCIATES; LABAN, DEPTFORD, LONDON, BY HERZOG & DE MEURON; THE SPACE, DUNDEE COLLEGE, BY NICHOLL RUSSELL STUDIOS; WHITBY VISITOR CENTRE, BY STANTON WILLIAMS

The winner of the 2003 ADAPT Trust Access Award was
THE SPACE, DUNDEE COLLEGE

45 .THE ADAPT TRUST ACCESS AWARD

THE SPACE, DUNDEE COLLEGE
.DUNDEE .NICHOLL RUSSELL STUDIOS

The brief for Dundee College's new centre for dance and drama projects was complex: to provide a base for professional contemporary-dance training and performance, and to provide an accessible and welcoming venue for local people.

Instead of applying facilities for people with a variety of disabilities retrospectively, as is so often the case, here all the thinking has gone on well in advance, with continuous consultation with access specialists and local groups. It could even be said to be the starting point for the project. From the closely placed designated parking spaces (or convenient drop-off point) to the easy-to-open doors, the clear and elegant signage and obvious routes both in and out, the well-designed lifts, an auditorium with the flexibility to deal with late bookings from wheelchair users, and the excellent acoustics – everything is designed to be inclusive and to make for a welcoming and enjoyable experience for people of all abilities. The same goes for behind the scenes with good access to backstage, the control room and even the operational fly galleries. This is a scheme which goes well beyond what is statutorily required.

From the moment the visitor sets eyes on the new buildings they present an irrepressibly vibrant image. A triangular auditorium points its prow towards the visitor, and its dark metallic-grey-painted concrete walls are lined on one side by the jaunty, curvaceous forms of overlapping metal screens, giving it a touch of the Bilbaos. Inside the building, a full-height foyer wraps around the auditorium, and the dancing metal screens continue through without interruption to culminate in a courtyard at the rear, used for impromptu performances. Big glass doors separate the public reception areas from a student 'buzz' area to the rear, with its heated floor where dancers can relax and 'warm-down' after exercise.

The ADAPT Trust also commends the shortlisted entries, Hampstead Theatre, Laban, and especially Whitby Abbey Visitor Centre, where the access problems of a historic site have been elegantly and practically solved.

CLIENT DUNDEE COLLEGE
THEATRE CONSULTANT SANDY BROWN ASSOCIATES
STRUCTURAL ENGINEER WSP STRUCTURES
SERVICES ENGINEER WSP SERVICES
CONTRACTOR TORITH LTD
COST £3.35 MILLION
PHOTOGRAPHER KEITH HUNTER

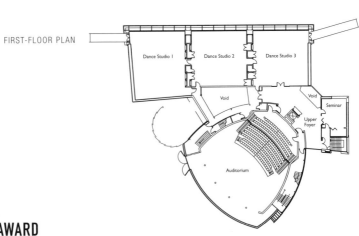

FIRST-FLOOR PLAN

Dance Studio 1   Dance Studio 2   Dance Studio 3

Void

Void

Seminar

Upper
Foyer

Auditorium

47 .THE ADAPT TRUST ACCESS AWARD

THE ARCHITECTS' JOURNAL FIRST BUILDING AWARD

The Architects' Journal First Building Award, worth £5,000, is given for an architect's first stand-alone building and is sponsored by *The Architects' Journal* with Robin Ellis Design and Construction. Previous winners have been Cedar House in Logiealmond, and Barnhouse in Highgate.

It requires courage for an architect to set up on their own after seven years training plus, often several more in the relatively safe environment of a bigger practice. As well as guts, it needs a lucky break, which ideally means finding a great client. All of this year's shortlisted architects found sympathetic and imaginative clients.

The Architects' Journal, founded in 1895, is the premier paid-for UK architectural weekly. Robin Ellis Design and Construction, the award's co-sponsors, were recently responsible for key parts of the refurbishment of the RIBA's Headquarters in Portland Place, London.

The 2003 shortlist was
ABERDEEN LANE, LONDON N1, BY AZMAN OWENS ARCHITECTS; NO. 1 CENTAUR STREET, LONDON SE1, BY DE RIJKE MARSH MORGAN; COWLEY MANOR HOTEL AND SPA, GLOUCESTERSHIRE, BY DE MATOS STOREY RYAN; THINK TANK, WEST IRELAND, BY GUMUCHDJIAN ARCHITECTS

The winner of the 2003 Architects' Journal First Building supported by Robin Ellis Design and Construction was
NO. 1 CENTAUR STREET, LONDON SE1

NO. 1 CENTAUR STREET
.LONDON SE1 .DE RIJKE MARSH MORGAN

This project is the product of a collaboration between an intelligent and brave client and an intelligent and brave architect. The site is initially unpromising, set between a railway arch on one side and a row of listed buildings on the other, leading to acoustic and planning constraints. But as in many of the best buildings, constraints have prompted innovative solutions borne out of lateral thinking. Most striking is the use of in-situ concrete as both structure and internal finish, giving both physical protection (from noise) and psychological protection (from the ravages of the city beyond).

Concrete also allows flexibility in the spatial solution for the interiors. The obvious approach would have been to stack up four floors of repetitive loft-type space. Instead, the client and architect devised a more innovative system of two-storey apartments on the ground floor with three-storey apartments over, leading to a spatial (and social) richness. To achieve this sense of spatial delight in a one-off house would have been commendable – to get it on a tight urban site for speculative private housing is really remarkable. The north-facing apartments have winter gardens, double-height spaces of glassy luxury. And best of all are the roof decks that sit at the same level as the main railway lines curving out of Waterloo, with Big Ben glimpsed beyond – an intense London experience under big skies.

Materially, the project demonstrates the architects' research into new building materials – everyday, prefabricated, and often surprising. The exterior is clad in a rainscreen made out of woodgrained fibrous-cement boards, usually employed for North American kit houses. It sounds tacky, but in the way it is detailed and spaced, the cladding feels completely appropriate for the toughness of the site. Elsewhere, the roughness of the in-situ concrete is juxtaposed with rich linings of walnut veneer, the latter imbuing the former with a certain luxury.

This is a project that pushes at the edges of architecture both materially and spatially. It breaks all the normal rules of decorum and refinement and is all the better for that.

CLIENT SOLID SPACE DEVELOPMENT LTD
STRUCTURAL ENGINEER ADAMS, KARA, TAYLOR
LANDSCAPE ARCHITECT JENNY COE LANDSCAPE ARCHITECTS
QS AZ URBAN STUDIO
CONTRACTOR PARKWAY CONSTRUCTION
COST £1 MILLION
PHOTOGRAPHER MICHAEL MACK

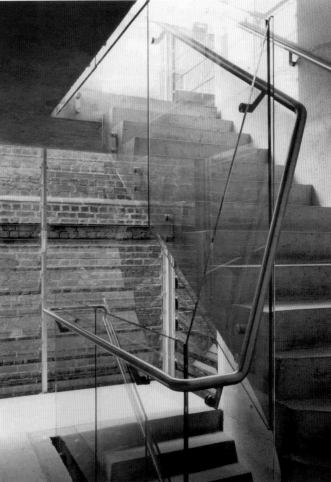

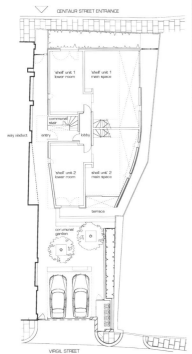

GROUND-FLOOR PLAN

THE CROWN ESTATE CONSERVATION AWARD

The Crown Estate Conservation Award is made to the architects of the best work of conservation that demonstrates successful restoration and/or adaptation of an architecturally significant building. It carries a prize of £5000. Previous winners have included Peter Inskip and Peter Jenkins for the Temple of Concord and Victory, Foster & Partners for The Reichstag and the JC Decaux UK Headquarters, Rick Mather Architects for the Dulwich Picture Gallery and, last year, Richard Murphy Architects with Simpson Brown Architects for the Stirling Tolbooth.

The Crown Estate manages a large and uniquely diverse portfolio of land and buildings across the UK. One of its primary concerns is to make historic buildings suitable to the needs of today's users.

The 2003 shortlist was
BLACKWELL, THE ARTS AND CRAFTS HOUSE, BOWNESS-ON-WINDERMERE, BY ALLIES AND MORRISON; COWLEY MANOR HOTEL AND SPA, GLOUCESTERSHIRE, BY DE MATOS STOREY RYAN; NEWHAILES HOUSE CONSERVATION, MUSSELBURGH, BY LDN ARCHITECTS; WHITBY ABBEY VISITOR CENTRE, BY STANTON WILLIAMS

The winner of the 2003 Crown Estate Conservation Award was
NEWHAILES HOUSE CONSERVATION, MUSSELBURGH

53 .THE CROWN ESTATE CONSERVATION AWARD

NEWHAILES HOUSE CONSERVATION
.MUSSELBURGH .LDN ARCHITECTS

Newhailes is a national treasure and deserves to be treated with the same care as would be given to an important painting or sculpture. The conservation plan placed any changes in the context of the whole rather than treating any element in isolation. The principle adhered to throughout was to do as much as necessary and as little as possible.

Law & Dunbar-Naismith's contribution to the minimalist preservation of grade A-listed 17th-century Newhailes House lies at the cutting edge of building-conservation theory. The house, with its fabric, decorations, fittings and contents dating back to all the periods of its four-century existence, was acquired in 1995 by the National Trust for Scotland. After extensive research, the Trust decided to preserve the house as found, with all its mellow ageing, rather than heavily restore it to some selected date in the past. Unsafe balustrades were refixed but their peeling paintwork was left untouched pending redecoration at some later date. Bowed floors were checked for structural integrity and further movement simply inhibited. This policy of conservation rather than restoration has shocked some visitors, more used to the brightness of conventional restoration.

Much of the key conservation work is all but invisible, such as the installation of electrics, heating, disabled access, fire detectors and sprinklers. The use of radio telemetry helps reduce the amount of wiring in the principal rooms and enables the fire brigade to pinpoint a fire source with uncanny accuracy. But backstage, these services are exposed, following the routes of Victorian plumbing and gas pipes; the alternative would have been to hack at plaster in order to bury them.

The family regarded themselves as stewards rather than owners of Newhailes, declining creature comforts such as central heating because of the damage such changes would cause. The National Trust for Scotland continues to take the same line: that to replace anything is to take away from the past.

CLIENT THE NATIONAL TRUST FOR SCOTLAND
STRUCTURAL ENGINEER ELLIOTT & COMPANY
SERVICES ENGINEER IRONS FOULNER CONSULTING ENGINEERS
LANDSCAPE ARCHITECT PETER MCGOWAN ASSOCIATES
QS JOHN DANSKEN & PURDIE
CONTRACTOR LINFORD BRIDGEMAN
COST £4.8 MILLION
PHOTOGRAPHER NATIONAL TRUST FOR SCOTLAND

THE MANSER MEDAL 2003

All the RIBA Award-winning one-off houses and major extensions in the UK were considered for this year's Manser Medal and four were shortlisted. The winner was announced at the RIBA Awards Dinner in June.

Custom Publishing, publishers of *Planahome*, which has been running the National HomeBuilder Design Awards for 23 years, with the aim of improving the standards of developers' schemes by encouraging them to use good architects, established the Manser Medal to reward the best one-off house in this country. It is named in honour of former RIBA President Michael Manser, himself the designer of a number of seminal houses. In 2003 the medal was made a part of the RIBA Awards, with entries drawn from schemes winning RIBA Awards in that year.

The 2003 shortlist was
ABERDEEN LANE, LONDON N1, BY AZMAN OWENS ARCHITECTS; ANDERSON HOUSE, LONDON W1, BY JAMIE FOBERT ARCHITECTS; THE PAVILION, NEW MALTINGS, NAYLAND, SUFFOLK, BY KNOX BHAVAN ARCHITECTS; THE RED HOUSE, CHELSEA, BY TONY FRETTON ARCHITECTS

The winner of the 2003 Manser Medal was
ANDERSON HOUSE, LONDON W1

ANDERSON HOUSE
.LONDON W1 .JAMIE FOBERT ARCHITECTS

What was formerly an inaccessible, valueless hole in the ground now has considerable real-estate value and is an iconic, comfortable and elegant architectural pad in a classy part of London. It takes your breath away and, now it is done, it seems so simple and so obvious. The architect's fee is a derisory part of its overall value. The client also deserves a medal.

Hidden within the centre of a residential block, enclosed on all sides by 7-metre-high party walls, the proposal to insert a house into this void was ambitious, imaginative and patently a challenge. Originally built as a small bakery, the site was last used as a shoe factory in the early part of the last century. It is entered through a 1-metre-wide passage between adjacent buildings. This leads into a small open space where two derelict buildings stood – the original three-storey workshop and a small 1930s' addition. These were demolished. The new works then required 26 separate Party Wall Agreements, 60 Party Wall Notices and 8 Party Wall Surveyors. It was worth it – this project is a gem.

The client wanted a house that embodied solidity and light, volume and texture, a house that resolved the difficulties of the site – its long, narrow access and the windowless perimeter – with a simple solution rather than added complexity. The planners stipulated that the existing envelope could not be exceeded. Indeed, the planning constraints are probably the single biggest contributor to the innovative solution conceived by the architect. As the new house could not rely on party walls, the majority of the load is carried on a central pile cap from which the concrete structure rises to form the principal walls of the interior, stairs and ceiling of the first floor. All three processes of structure, wall and finish are resolved in this single material.

This project is a shining example of how an innovative, contemporary and spatially aware architecture can be constructed in the heart of a conservation area.

CLIENT PRIVATE
STRUCTURAL ENGINEER MICHAEL BARCLAY PARTNERSHIP
QS BOYDEN & COMPANY
CONTRACTOR HORGAN BROTHERS LTD
COST £402,000
PHOTOGRAPHER DAVID GRANDORGE

GROUND-FLOOR PLAN

59 .THE MANSER MEDAL

THE RIBA CLIENT OF THE YEAR

The RIBA set up the Client of the Year Award six years ago and, apart from the Stirling Prize and the Royal Gold Medal, it is the most important award the Institute makes. Unless the people who commission buildings have vision and faith, there can be no good architecture. Everyone has benefited from the taste and persistence of good clients, from the Medicis to Roland Paoletti.

Arts Council England once again supported the award, as it has done from the start. The prize is £5,000, to be spent on a contemporary work of art by an artist working in Britain. In this way the prize supports good architects and good artists.

Architecture is a team effort and previous winners have amply demonstrated that: Roland Paoletti, who received the first award for the new Jubilee Line stations; The MCC for commissioning a series of fine buildings at Lord's Cricket Ground; the Foreign and Commonwealth Office for pulling off a series of iconic embassies around the world; the Moledinar Park Housing Association Glasgow for its campus of buildings by a variety of Scottish architects; and Urban Splash for its commitment both to design quality and the regeneration of Manchester and Liverpool.

The 2003 shortlist – together with 2002–3 RIBA Award-winning, cited schemes – was
CAMBRIDGE UNIVERSITY – CENTRE FOR MATHEMATICAL SCIENCES; GATESHEAD – BALTIC: CENTRE FOR CONTEMPORARY ART AND GATESHEAD MILLENNIUM BRIDGE; LABAN – LABAN, DEPTFORD; THE PEABODY TRUST – BEDZED; MANCHESTER CITY COUNCIL – CITY ART GALLERY, URBIS, INTERNATIONAL CONVENTION CENTRE

The winner of the 2003 RIBA Client of the Year was
MANCHESTER CITY COUNCIL

MANCHESTER CITY COUNCIL

Manchester City Council has been an exemplary client and enabler of good architecture, both directly and indirectly, for the last decade. As a result of what its chief executive Howard Bernstein has described as 'positive discrimination in favour of quality outcomes', the city has transformed its architectural and public-realm identity through a series of projects including the Commonwealth Stadium (now home to Manchester City football club), the expanded City Art Gallery, Urbis, the upgraded Piccadilly Station, and public-realm programmes including Piccadilly Gardens and the Castlefield area. The response to the bombing of the city centre has been to embrace good-quality design by both local and national architects, a policy that is now extending to the renewal of post-industrial regeneration sites in east Manchester. The council has provided an inspiring example of civic leadership echoing the spirit in which the city fathers created the great architectural landmarks of the 19th century, and is a more than worthy winner of this year's award.

This year alone the City Art Gallery, Urbis and Piccadilly Station (for Network Rail) have won RIBA Awards. In previous years as clients Manchester City Council has won RIBA awards with Manchester International Convention Centre (2002), Bridgewater Hall and Hulme Arch Bridge (both 1998); doubtless there will be more in the future. It has also helped facilitate many more RIBA award winners: post-bomb schemes for Marks & Spencer and the Corporation Street Footbridge (for Prudential) (both 2000), and numerous housing schemes for Urban Splash, Crosby Homes, the Irwell Valley Housing Association and the Guinness Trust.

THE RIBA JOURNAL SUSTAINABILITY AWARD

This prize, supported by *The RIBA Journal*, is made to the building which demonstrates most elegantly and durably the principles of sustainable architecture. The award is about building for future generations without destroying the world they will grow up in and is given in recognition of the importance of sustainability in architecture today. The prize was established in 2000 when the winner was Chetwood Associates' Sainsbury's at Greenwich. The other winners have been Michael Hopkins and Partners' Jubilee Campus, University of Nottingham and, last year, The Cardboard Building, Westborough Primary School, Westcliff-on-Sea by Cottrell + Vermeulen Architecture. This year's jury included Eric Parry, Guy Battle, Brian Vermeulen and Amanda Baillieu.

The RIBA Journal is published monthly by the Builder Group and was recently voted by RIBA members as the most important benefit of membership.

The 2003 shortlist was
BEDZED, WALLINGTON, BY BILL DUNSTER ARCHITECTS; BIOLOGICAL RESEARCH LABORATORIES, BIBERACH, GERMANY, BY SAUERBRUCH HUTTON; CENTRE FOR MATHEMATICAL SCIENCES, CAMBRIDGE, BY EDWARD CULLINAN ARCHITECTS; LOWESTOFT WASTE WATER WORKS, SUFFOLK, BY BARBER CASANOVAS RUFFLES; OFFALY COUNTY COUNCIL CIVIC OFFICES, IRELAND, BY ABK ARCHITECTS

The winner of the 2003 RIBA Journal Sustainability Award was
BEDZED, WALLINGTON, SURREY

BEDZED

Sustainability covers a wide range of issues affecting the environmental impact of a building. This year, as well looking for an approach to delivering sustainable systems for transportation, energy, water, waste, materials and community issues, The RIBA Journal Sustainability Award jury was also looking for buildings that pushed the sustainable agenda through a step change and took a more radical approach.

For this reason they were unanimous in their decision to award the prize to BedZED solar urban village, the mixed development on a brownfield site in Sutton, south London. While other schemes the judges considered were varying shades of green, BedZED goes way beyond the standard environmental checklist by challenging both the way we live and work. The near carbon-neutral lifestyle at BedZED is, of course, only achievable if there are sustainable technologies to support it and people willing to buy into a very different way of life from the one most of us are used to. Until now, pioneering communities have only been attained at the expense of architectural ambition, but at BedZED the architects have been highly innovative. Although the development is dense, each unit has its own external space, while the flats themselves have very high levels of daylight, making modest space standards appear more generous and airy. The judges were also impressed by BedZED's long-term goal, which is to see our urban habitat transformed to carbon-neutral mixed-use development by the end of the century. Finally, this is far more than simply a demonstration project for the sustainability message; it is a powerful incentive for the housing industry to change its ways of thinking and building.

For building description and other judges' comments see pages 22–25.

THE STEPHEN LAWRENCE PRIZE

The Stephen Lawrence Prize, sponsored by The Goldschmied Foundation, was set up in 1998 to draw attention to the kind of creativity architects have to display when working on low budgets. It is awarded to the architect of an RIBA Award-winning building costing less than £350,000. The prize commemorates Stephen Lawrence, the black teenager who was just setting out on the road to becoming an architect when he was murdered in south London in 1993.

The Goldschmied Foundation, established by RIBA Past President Marco Goldschmied, supports the Stephen Lawrence Charitable Trust and, in particular, its bursary programme. The winning architect of the Stephen Lawrence Prize receives a cheque for £5,000. A further £5,000 funds a bursary to help train young black architects.

The 2003 shortlist was
MOAT HOUSE, DORSINGTON, BY GLENN HOWELLS ARCHITECTS; PRIVATE HOUSE IN GALICIA, SPAIN, BY DAVID CHIPPERFIELD ARCHITECTS WITH CARLOS SEOANE; THINK TANK, WEST IRELAND, BY GUMUCHDJIAN ARCHITECTS; YOUNG HOUSE, LONDON W11, BY TONKIN LIU

The winner of the 2003 Stephen Lawrence Prize was
THINK TANK, WEST IRELAND

THINK TANK
.SKIBBERREEN, IRELAND .GUMUCHDJIAN ARCHITECTS

Set on the banks of the River Ilen, near the town of Skibberreen in West Cork, the building was conceived as a cross between a thinker's retreat and a bird-watcher's hide. The architectural references are to both boat-houses and barns. The design resolves these references into a simple expression of roof, frame and screens, making it appear timeless, almost a 'found' object in a stunning landscape. The openness of the structure is tempered by cedar slatted screens which provide shade and contain the views.

The judges described it as a sophisticated yet primitive hut. It very successfully fuses the tradition of vernacular building with detailing that is more normally associated with the fashion industry. The design process was an excellent collaborative effort between the local builder, with his knowledge of materials and weathering, the well-informed vision of the architect, the London-based specialist contractor and an unerring sense of simple decorum on the part of the client.

The materials were selected to juxtapose 'stable' elements, such as glass and stainless steel, with materials that weather, like the cedar roof planks, slats and decking. There is a lot of constructional invention that would be appreciated by architectural theorists from Laugier to Rykwert. The low walls and the overhanging cedar roof provide physical and psychological shelter from the volatile weather with its sudden and dramatic storms, while the transparency of the glazed wall panels sets the occupier within this most beautiful riparine setting. The hybrid structure of timber encased steel piers and timber roof trusses and edge beams speaks of a close dialogue between engineer and architect in the struggle to create a simple, timeless object.

ALSO SHORTLISTED FOR THE ARCHITECTS' JOURNAL FIRST BUILDING AWARD

CLIENT PRIVATE
STRUCTURAL ENGINEER BURO HAPPOLD
LANDSCAPE ARCHITECT VERNEY NAYLOR
CONTRACTORS BILL WOLFE / DMI
COST £200,000
PHOTOGRAPHER PHILIP GUMUCHDJIAN

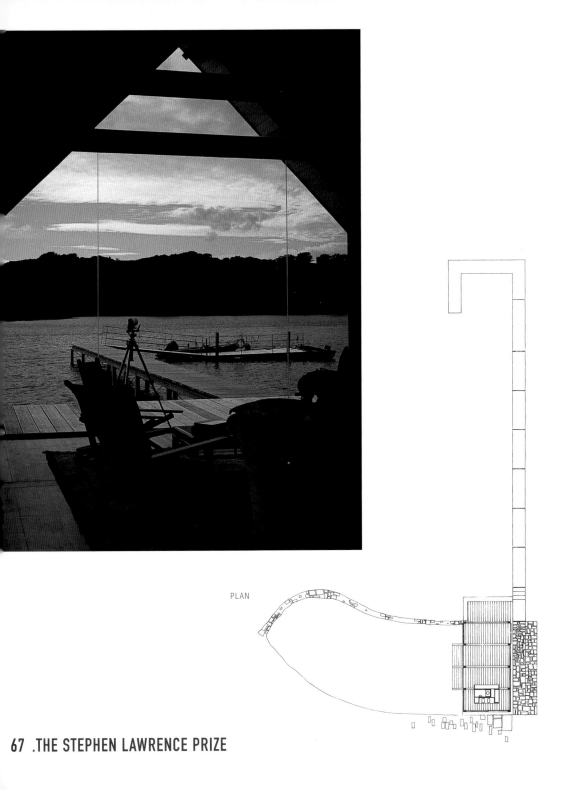

PLAN

THE RIBA AWARDS

THE RIBA AWARDS 2003

RIBA Awards are given for excellence rather than size or complexity. Jurors are encouraged to include buildings that are otherwise unlikely to come to public notice. Awards are judged regionally by a series of panels consisting of an architect of national renown (not from that region), a local architect, and a non-architect (the lay juror).

This section illustrates and describes, geographically from north to south, all of the winners which did not also win additional prizes or were not shortlisted for the RIBA Stirling Prize. These are shown elsewhere in this book.

Each winner is presented with certificates for the client, key consultants and contractor at ceremonies throughout the 14 RIBA regions. They also receive a lead plaque to affix to the building. These have been produced by The Lead Sheet Association for 12 years and the RIBA is grateful for the association's continuing support.

HARVEY NICHOLS RESTAURANT
.EDINBURGH .LIFSCHUTZ DAVIDSON

In the heart of Edinburgh's New Town, the new Harvey Nichols Forth Floor restaurant has spectacular views stretching from the castle to the Firth of Forth and includes an 85-cover restaurant, a 90-cover brasserie and almost 280 square metres of food market and kitchen shop. The restaurant is closest to the terrace, giving it the best views; the brasserie is just behind, separated by moveable glass screens; a bar serving both is at the centre of the plan. During store opening hours, escalators emerge in the food market, meaning that diners can see the produce that will make up their meal; at night they are brought directly into the restaurant by lift.

This is an exhilaratingly stylish, witty and sumptuous fit-out. Materials are chosen for their intrinsic quality and durability. The warmth and textures of surfaces are attuned to location and use, so timber for the intimate restaurant, bar and reception desks and stainless steel for the food store and display units; the floor of the retail area is of cool Carrara marble, the restaurant areas use European oak parquet.

The scene is set by a dense grid of 150 circular ceiling recesses that are top lit. They change gradually from bright orange at twilight to a low red glow later in the evening. Other inspired touches include a reception desk with echoes of art deco, toilets lined with narrow translucent glass tiles and carefully positioned mirrors, and lifts lined in patterned polished stainless steel. An outdoor terrace sheltered by a projecting roof canopy caters for al-fresco dining. The coloured ceiling lights along with the row of reflective light bulbs above the outdoor terrace add spectacle to St Andrew's Square below.

CLIENT HARVEY NICHOLS REGIONAL STORES
STRUCTURAL ENGINEER ARUP
SERVICES ENGINEER ARUP
QS E C HARRIS
CONTRACTOR ANDBRIDGE LTD
COST £1.78 MILLION
PHOTOGRAPHER CHRIS GASCOIGNE

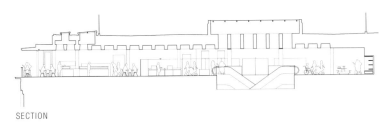

SECTION

JACK KILBY COMPUTER CENTRE, NAPIER UNIVERSITY
.EDINBURGH .RICHARD MURPHY ARCHITECTS

At Napier University, Richard Murphy was asked to design a 24-hour-access computer centre at the heart of the Merchiston Campus, providing accommodation not only for 500 workstations but also support space for technical staff, for the main servers and ancillary accommodation. The project also involved the refurbishment of the surrounding buildings. Overall, it gives the computer centre a visual presence on the campus that was previously a series of unremarkable interiors.

How many computer rooms have we seen in which serried ranks of operators work in artificial light and air, sandwiched between a fake ceiling and a raised floor? Here, in what were the heavy-engineering workshops, a large open-plan computer hall seats 500 with no clear subdivision or obviously marked circulation routes. The architects have introduced two strong elements that humanize this environment, even though there are no external walls offering the opportunity for windows. Firstly, the floor rises in a stepped hillside of four terraces, with the plant tucked below the upper levels. Secondly, the roof is divided into five parallel barrel vaults running perpendicular to the terracing and supported on clusters of four columns. The combined effect is to break up the huge, potentially daunting hall into 20 distinct bays. Natural daylight is channelled in through clerestory windows at the bases of the barrel vaults, and this is bounced upwards by metal reflectors and down off the white-painted vaults into the hall below. Combined with a finely modulated colour scheme, shafts of sunlight at key points, and well-tuned artificial light, this produces a wonderful, calm workspace that has become very popular with students.

Once again, Richard Murphy has pulled off the trick of making a very special place out of an unpromising brief.

CLIENT NAPIER UNIVERSITY
STRUCTURAL ENGINEER W S ATKINS
SERVICES ENGINEER W S ATKINS
QS FAITHFUL & GOULD
PROJECT MANAGER BOVIS LEND LEASE
CONTRACTOR OGILVIE CONSTRUCTION
COST £4.5 MILLION
PHOTOGRAPHER ALAN FORBES

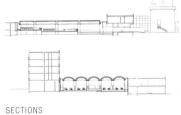

SECTIONS

WADDELL HOUSE
.POLLOCKSHIELDS, GLASGOW .STUDIO KAP

The house lies in a garden suburb of Glasgow – a conservation area – and is a proud, four-square blond sandstone villa with extensive grounds. The architects were called in initially to solve a mundane problem: alterations to the attics by previous owners did not comply with building regulations; but, as so often much bigger aspirations emerged during discussions between architect and clients. As a result, the project involved substantial remodelling of the back of the house to provide a new living space, kitchen and utility areas, a study, and a terrace overlooking the garden. Major work was also undertaken on the ground floor of the existing house, not only to upgrade it but also to improve its relationship with the new rooms. On the first floor, two new bathrooms and a dressing room were created and the stair to the top floor altered to allow more daylight into the attic rooms. Keen collectors of contemporary art, the clients also specified good hanging spaces; these too have been cleverly provided. The final result is far more than the sum of its parts.

The judges thought that the project combined an excellent architectural statement in its own right with a carefully composed connection to the original house. The modern single-storey extension is bounded on either side by the ashlar stone walls and corner chimney breast of the house's original rear extension. Above the old walls floats a new flat roof in stainless steel. This is raised above clerestory windows and projects at the garden end to cover a porch. Looking back from this porch, a long enfilade of rooms is revealed, uniting new extension with old house. The whole design is a fine composition of balanced contrasts.

CLIENTS ANDREW AND JO WADDELL
STRUCTURAL ENGINEER: WOOLGAR HUNTER STRUCTURAL ENGINEERS
QS REID FLETCHER
CONTRACTOR C & V CONSTRUCTION
COST £170,000
PHOTOGRAPHER KEITH HUNTER

SITE PLAN

WESTPORT PROJECT, EVOLUTION HOUSE .EDINBURGH .REIACH & HALL ARCHITECTS

Because Edinburgh straddles a number of hills, its buildings work on many levels. This remarkable scheme for lettable, open-plan speculative offices is made up of a series of stepped terraces providing a variety of viewing platforms for occupants, and for those on the outside a welcome visual break of horizontal layers in the vertical, even vertiginous Old Town. The building adopts a positive, responsive and realistic attitude to energy conservation and this is expressed in its appearance. The structure is exposed to act as a heat sink; solar gain is reduced by incorporating external sliding screens on the south and east façades. The low-energy strategy also involves the adoption of a displacement ventilation system in place of conventional air-conditioning. Throughout, good design has given add-on value without additional over-the-odds costs.

It is rare to find an office building that combines so well the generality of a flexible office brief with the particular demands of a very special site. The building sits on a corner at an asymmetrical crossroads, with the glorious castle, floodlit at night, hovering close above it.

The lifts, stairs and services are arranged in a cool and graceful straight line that stretches the length of the plan. The office space, which is column-free, occupies the space between this line and the peculiarly shaped outer edge of the site. This allows the elevations (of stone, glass and metal shades) to respond to the particular edge conditions with good articulation, and the plans of the offices to be both special and as efficient as possible. It is a graceful solution to a very tricky task.

CLIENT AMA (NEW TOWN) LTD
STRUCTURAL ENGINEER SKM KIRKMAN + BRADFORD
CONTRACTOR HBG CONSTRUCTION
COST £7.6 MILLION
PHOTOGRAPHER GAVIN FRASER

79 .SCOTLAND

WOLFSON MEDICAL SCHOOL, UNIVERSITY OF GLASGOW
.GLASGOW .REIACH & HALL ARCHITECTS

Glasgow University's new Wolfson Medical School building celebrates 550 years of the city's university and stems from competition-winning designs that were developed in consultation with the users. The result is a crystalline minimalist glass envelope with a projecting second glass skin. The architectural concept – three articulated blocks arranged round a triangular atrium – responds well to the firm's masterplan for the whole site and to the urban landscape of the West End of Glasgow as a whole.

This is a well-considered response to a prominent triangular site just down the hill from the university's neo-gothic landmark building. Pride of place at the apex of the site has been given to the school's computerized library, now called the study landscape area, which occupies the upper three floors behind a curved triple-skinned glass façade. The other external walls are clad in simple white render, though sandstone facings have been attached to one side to relate to the houses opposite. The building's greatest delight is on the inside, where the three wings of accommodation have been gathered around a triangular atrium that is beautifully top-lit through a glass roof supported on glass beams with a record-breaking 16-metre span. Teaching and ancillary accommodation is intelligently arranged around the atrium, and detailing is consistently lean and solid in this well-balanced building. The landscaping has created a series of new public spaces that help to integrate university and city.

Writing last year in the *Scotsman*, the dean of the school summed up his feelings: 'If you can provide people with a lovely working environment, why not? Perhaps this building has stretched the medical school's horizons. We didn't imagine you could create such a beautiful building with such prosaic functions.'

CLIENT THE UNIVERSITY OF GLASGOW
STRUCTURAL ENGINEER URS CORPORATION
SERVICES ENGINEER HULLEY & KIRKWOOD
QS TURNER & TOWNSEND
CONTRACTOR COSTAIN LTD
COST £9 MILLION
PHOTOGRAPHER GAVIN FRASER

81 .SCOTLAND

EDEL MCELHOLME OPTICIANS
.DOWNPATRICK .WHITE INK ARCHITECTS

Downpatrick is a tired, sleepy 18th- and 19th-century town, reputedly the birthplace of St Patrick, but it retains some of the scars of Northern Ireland's Troubles, most obviously a paucity of new investment in its buildings and environment. Edel McElholme's recently converted shop premises in Market Street come as something of a surprise and are a stunning demonstration of how good architecture can be created without a substantial budget and in an uninspiring and constrained context.

The architects had only the ground floor of a small 19th-century shop to work with, just 6 metres wide and stretching back 33 metres. Daylight was available only from the street frontage and a small courtyard formed at the rear. Nevertheless, the brief for Ms McElholme's new optician's shop required the provision of a showroom area, test rooms, a laboratory, lens-fitting rooms and a waiting area, offices and staff rooms.

The new internal spaces have all been set out along the side of a single wide circulation route that runs without interruption from the front shop door to the lens-fitting room at the rear, ramping up from the street to the main level to provide easy access for disabled users. Along the route the clever but discreet use of mirrors, combined with the creation of display bays whose rhythm is reflected in the polished flooring, and the controlled use of strong colour and lighting give both admirable clarity for users and drama.

Edel McElholme found her architect stimulating, practical and a pleasure to work with and directly attributes much of the success of her business since reopening to his design – interestingly, she notes that not only has the number of customers to the shop increased but they also seem to enjoy spending more. This excellent project demonstrates yet again how good design pays.

CLIENT MS EDEL MCELHOLME
STRUCTURAL ENGINEER P D SAVAGE + ASSOCIATES
CONTRACTOR JAMES HUGHES
COST £95,000
PHOTOGRAPHER TODD WILSON – SIGNALS

BALTIC: CENTRE FOR CONTEMPORARY ART
.GATESHEAD .ELLIS WILLIAMS

The transformation of Gateshead's Baltic Flour Mills into a world-class venue for the visual arts is an extraordinary achievement. The original building, designed in the 1930s but completed in the early 1950s, had a simple programme – the storage of thousands of tons of flour in 148 giant concrete silos on a site accessible by sea and land. The architecture was powerful, almost civic in character – a symmetrical composition on a gigantic scale dressed in a smart cloak of red and buff brick.

It was not an obvious idea to convert this massive honeycomb of explosion-resistant concrete and masonry into an art space in which the primary needs are floods of light and open access. But it was an inspired one. The project was driven by the ambition of the city of Gateshead as client, the vision of the director, Sune Nordgren, and the creativity of the architect and the engineering team.

The location is unbeatable and has been exploited magnificently by capturing the stunning views up, down and across the Tyne, most dramatically from the glazed lifts and projecting upper-floor galleries, and most surprisingly from the toilets on the top floor. The greatest challenge was to make an easily usable public building spread over six storeys. This has been achieved by the ingenious manipulation of the section which folds together galleries, art spaces, offices, library and restaurants in a way that constantly draws the visitor upwards. It is an astonishing achievement to make a building that seems so solid and enclosed from the outside feel so transparent from the inside.

So many uses demand space at ground level – including the money-making activities associated with arrival and departure, deliveries and large-scale storage. This problem has been solved by creating an elegant building that sits on the plaza in front of the original structure. Distinct in its language but entirely integrated with the geometry of the original, it provides a controlled and dramatic introduction to a stunning architectural experience.

CLIENT GATESHEAD COUNCIL
STRUCTURAL ENGINEER ATELIER ONE
SERVICES ENGINEER ATELIER TEN
QS BOYDEN & CO.
CONTRACTOR HBG CONSTRUCTION NORTH EAST
COST £37 MILLION
PHOTOGRAPHER ETIENNE CLÉMENT

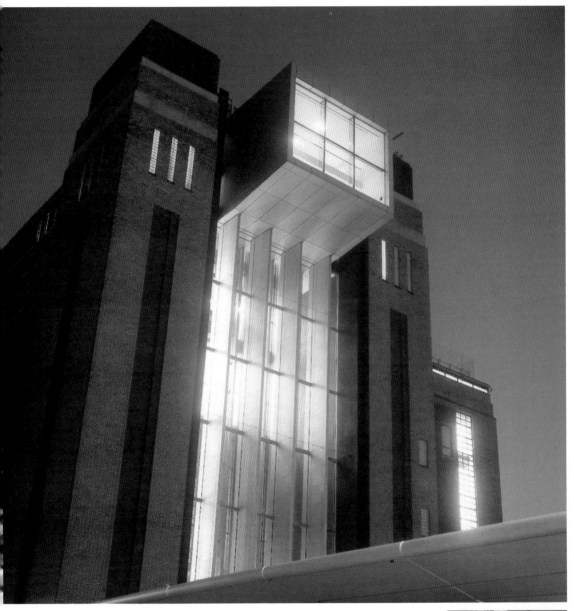

SECTION

BLACKWELL, THE ARTS AND CRAFTS HOUSE .BOWNESS-ON-WINDERMERE .ALLIES & MORRISON

This seminal arts-and-crafts holiday home on Lake Windermere, designed by M H Baillie Scott and built around 1900, has now been restored and adapted with great ingenuity and sensitivity. Built for the Manchester brewer Sir Edward Holt, the house had fallen into disrepair by the 1990s, having gone through lives as a boarding school and as offices. The brief called for the adaptation of the Grade I house into a gallery for the applied arts. An English Heritage architect was appointed to act as a Heritage Lottery Fund monitor. The aim was to retain Baillie Scott's 'soul of the artistic house' and its 'atmosphere of deep-seated calm', every bit as much as it was to reveal the wealth of arts-and-crafts details and the rich interior spaces. The gallery had to meet the tough requirements of the Museums and Galleries Commission for the housing of loan collections.

The skill of the architects on a project like this is as much in covering their tracks as in expressing new work where appropriate. In many of the major rooms of this lovely house the usual issues of accommodating fire doors, air-conditioning and security installations have been handled with great discretion, while the reorganisation of the entry, the provision of lift access and a new staircase have been designed with sensitivity and contemporary quality.

There is a balance to be achieved in expressing honestly the new work as being of our own time and and yet not jarring with the original. This balance has been well struck in this exemplar of conservation and reuse.

SHORTLISTED FOR THE CROWN ESTATE CONSERVATION AWARD

CLIENT LAKELAND ARTS TRUST
STRUCTURAL ENGINEER HARRIS & SUTHERLAND
SERVICES ENGINEER MAX FORDHAM & PARTNERS
LANDSCAPE ARCHITECT KIM WILKIE ASSOCIATES
QS BOYDEN & COMPANY
CONTRACTOR WILLIAM ANELAY LTD
COST £1.5 MILLION
PHOTOGRAPHER CHARLOTTE WOOD

BOXWORKS
.MANCHESTER .ARKHEION

Boxworks is a cornerstone of the Britannia Basin development and a key part of the regeneration of the whole of east Manchester. A former cardboard factory, it is now 83 shell apartments – the first in Manchester.

This is the second major transformation the building has undergone. In the 1920s it was given an art-deco façade and this element has now become the main feature to be preserved, set against new elevations of steel and glass that overlay the original building. Internally, the circulation is dramatic with lift access giving panoramic views; and then a bright internal street, five storeys high, with a single wall of plywood within which apartment entrances are subtly accommodated, and off which comes a magically lit internal corridor, confounding expectations. The planning of the apartments themselves is complex, inventive and well executed.

Urban Splash teamed up with Granada TV to choose three architects to produce ideas for turning individual shells into show lofts. One resulted in the Naked Loft, which places a glass bathroom at the heart of the apartment, partially etched to disguise services and with aluminium curtains affording privacy. Rooms are divided using huge storage walls or voile curtains.

Protected in the L-shaped plan from the outside environment is a communal garden, primarily of hard landscaping, which is also inventive and well made. The penthouse flat for the developer is not unexpectedly a *tour de force*. Looking out from this luxurious apartment to the sea of dereliction all around underlines the spirit of adventure of both client and architect in investing in this part of the city.

CLIENT URBAN SPLASH
STRUCTURAL ENGINEER WHITBYBIRD
SERVICES ENGINEER BURO HAPPOLD
QS SIMON FENTON PARTNERSHIP
CONTRACTOR URBAN SPLASH PROJECTS
COST £7.95 MILLION
PHOTOGRAPHER PHOTOFLEX

CHORLTON PARK HOUSING
.MANCHESTER .STEPHENSON BELL

Irwell Valley Housing Association ran an invited competition to design 20 shared-ownership flats to be built on the contaminated site of a petrol station. Urban Splash's Tom Bloxham, one of the judges, suggested a joint venture in which seven premium apartments for outright sale would be added to the scheme. Most of the scheme is at three storeys, though one element of five storeys pushes the timber-frame construction to its structural limits. The building has low embodied energy, is highly insulated, quiet and warm.

The site is on the corner of a major and minor road in an unremarkable landscape of inter-war semi-detached housing. Three storeys of steel-mesh-floored external balconies, supported on a heroic timber trellis structure, make a very unusual but very successful external façade to an otherwise unspectacularly planned housing scheme. The inside of the L-shape of the development is a remarkably quiet communal garden. This sits on top of the very generous underground car parking made from the petrol tanks of the filling station formerly on the site.

Access is by generous decks (giving the lie to the myth that it is impossible to do successful deck-access housing), and the clever combination of homes for sale on the top floors with housing-association flats underneath has led to a very high specification for all and a very welcome mix of owner occupiers and tenants. Allied to this are some remarkable energy statistics, achieved without the use of photovoltaics and the like, just sensible high levels of insulation and good whole-house ventilation, leading to heating costs of less than £100 per house per year.

CLIENT IRWELL VALLEY HOUSING ASSOCIATION
STRUCTURAL ENGINEER WHITBYBIRD
SERVICES ENGINEER STEVEN A HUNT & ASSOCIATES
QS SIMON FENTON PARTNERSHIP
CONTRACTOR MCGOFF AND BYRNE
COST £1.75 MILLION
PHOTOGRAPHER CHARLOTTE WOOD

NO. 1 DEANSGATE
.MANCHESTER .IAN SIMPSON ARCHITECTS

No. 1 Deansgate is the most visible part of the city-centre rebuilding strategy proposed by Ian Simpson Architects after the 1996 IRA bomb. This landmark building has brought a new way of living to a city where previously apartments were all conversions. Crosby Homes has commissioned the tallest steel-framed residential building in the UK. A fully glazed tower is raised 9 metres above the retail podium by a raking steel structure. The accommodation block shows respect to the varying heights of its neighbours, and steps down towards the cathedral. The tower is double-skinned with each apartment having access via double-glazed doors to a semi-external space providing a flexible extension to the living accommodation. The outer skin is made up of openable louvres, which give the block its constantly shifting and shimmering appearance.

This project is an heroic symbol of the regeneration of Manchester's urban core, both formally, through its position at the crossing of Deansgate and St Mary's Gate, and psychologically, by putting housing so close to the city centre.

The building consists of 84 apartments on 14 floors levitated above the everyday world of the city street. The apartments are planned within the strict constraints of the structural-steel frame. An inventive and brilliant series of balconies is achieved through the tempered space with its external skin of louvred glass units.

Four rows of triple V-shaped legs support the apartment block via a transfer structure and this structural 'gap' in the building is filled by the generous apartment sky lobby. Below this is a retail podium, which adds to the historic bustle of Deansgate.

CLIENT CROSBY HOMES NW LTD
STRUCTURAL ENGINEER MARTIN STOCKLEY ASSOCIATES
SERVICES ENGINEER ROBERTS AND PARTNERS
QS DAVIS LANGDON & EVEREST
CONTRACTOR MACE
COST £20 MILLION
PHOTOGRAPHER PHOTEC

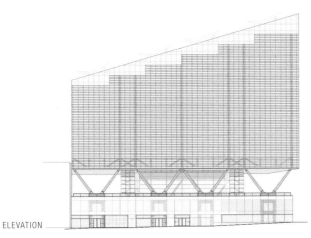

ELEVATION

93 .NORTH-WEST

MANCHESTER CITY ART GALLERY
.MANCHESTER .MICHAEL HOPKINS & PARTNERS

The extension and alteration of Manchester City Art Gallery was a large and complex project. It involved not only the construction of new galleries and the completion of a partially built city block, but also linking two existing buildings by Charles Barry: the Royal Manchester Institution and the Athenaeum. The former was already used as the City Art Gallery and the latter, previously a gentlemen's club, had been extended upwards to accommodate a theatre. Between the two buildings an alleyway bisected the block.

The architects have filled in the missing quarter of the city block and made a glazed link between the two halves. They have resisted the temptation to create a new entrance to the galleries, retaining instead the dignified entrance via the Ionic portico on to the main street. The old top-lit galleries, reached via a grand staircase, are all but untouched, but a glazed bridge leads from these, over the new link building into the new extension. This has its own grand stair, in glass, with two freestanding lift towers. Here the rooms match the sequence of rooms in the old gallery.

The new gallery and educational spaces are modern complements to Barry's originals and the link block is meticulously crafted and cleverly links the two. Indeed, the making of the whole building could not be faulted. The external façade is a classic example of the 'well-crafted container', successfully complementing both adjacent buildings.

MANCHESTER CITY COUNCIL SHORTLISTED FOR THE RIBA CLIENT OF THE YEAR

CLIENT MANCHESTER CITY COUNCIL
STRUCTURAL ENGINEER ARUP
SERVICES ENGINEER ARUP
QS GARDINER & THEOBALD
CONTRACTOR BOVIS LEND LEASE
COST £35 MILLION
PHOTOGRAPHER DENNIS GILBERT — VIEW

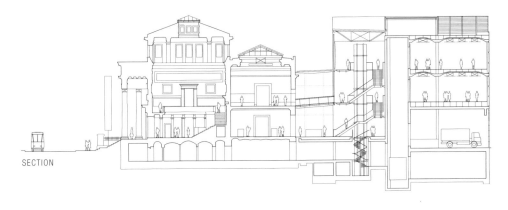

SECTION

95 .NORTH-WEST

MANCHESTER PICCADILLY STATION
.MANCHESTER .BUILDING DESIGN PARTNERSHIP

The transformation of Manchester Piccadilly Station represents the demise of one of the rail network's worst mainline terminals and its replacement with one of the best. The aim was to overcome the congestion problems experienced by passengers on the concourse and vehicles arriving at the station, and to create a suitable gateway for the city.

The hotch-potch of 1960s structures has been replaced with a steel-framed concourse building, an approach ramp, a taxi area, a multi-storey car park, and six storeys of train-crew accommodation. (A satellite lounge and travellator link are by other hands, working to BDP's masterplan.) The striking concourse roof is a combination of standing-seam aluminium and inflated ETFE pillows shaped to define the two main curving pedestrian routes through the complex. The steep monopitch roof is supported on a structure of steel bowstring trusses and provides approaching pedestrians with a clear marker.

While not pretending to be in the spectacular league of Milan or New York's Grand Central, the new pedestrian terminal fully complements the adjacent restored trainsheds, which are now airy and bright, probably for the first time since their construction. The scheme promotes ease of movement and provides easy accommodation of facilities and shopping. The general quality of design offers an atmosphere of comfort and reassurance, much closer to a superior sort of airport than that we have become used to at mainline stations. In particular, the radical and inspired reorganisation of the car and taxi arrangements, now housed in the vaults of the station, works brilliantly and is one of the few examples where a 'transport interchange' is a pleasure to use.

All this radical surgery was conducted while – in an extraordinary logistical exercise – the station continued to function.

CLIENT NETWORK RAIL
STRUCTURAL ENGINEER URS THORBURN COLQUHOUN
SERVICES ENGINEER BUILDING DESIGN PARTNERSHIP
TRAFFIC CONSULTANT FABER MAUNSELL
QS TURNER & TOWNSEND
CONTRACTOR LAING O'ROURKE
COST £60 MILLION
PHOTOGRAPHER DAVID BARBOUR

SECTION

TIMBER WHARF
.CASTLEFIELD, MANCHESTER .GLENN HOWELLS ARCHITECTS

Timber Wharf is Urban Splash's first entirely new-build residential scheme and it is done on an heroic scale. It was the subject of an RIBA competition in 1998 and is a response to the ambitious programme laid down by the Urban Task Force to bring high-density housing into our city centres. The brief called for contemporary apartments at a cost of less than £600 a square metre, using an innovative and environmentally friendly approach with materials and construction methods.

This is a dramatic, simple but elegant mixed housing and office project in a previously unfashionable corner of inner-city Manchester bordering the Bridgewater Canal. The area already houses Britannia Mills and Box Works. The simplicity of the repetitive precast-concrete façade has more connections with continental housing types than with established British examples. There is a heroic quality about the scheme seldom seem in the last decades of the 20th century, following the post-Ronan Point loss of political and architectural nerve. It is a brave and bold leap of faith for both the developer and the architect and in its early stages it shows every sign of success.

A variety of housing sizes and types have been accommodated within the repetitive structure; each is ingeniously planned and meticulously executed. The corners and tops of the buildings are reserved for special double-storey flats. On the ground floor are live/work, or just work units, which are adapted and used in a variety of ways. The single aesthetic of the precast-concrete cross walls expressed in all the interiors unites the whole project. In the centre a spectacular internal space around the lift core brings together the building from top to bottom and also provides a cleft in this wall-like structure, opening a view from the entrance elevation through to the canalside landscaping.

CLIENT URBAN SPLASH
STRUCTURAL ENGINEER MARTIN STOCKLEY ASSOCIATES
SERVICES ENGINEER BURO HAPPOLD
LANDSCAPE ARCHITECTS HYLAND EDGAR DRIVER / LANDSCAPE PROJECTS
QS SIMON FENTON PARTNERSHIP
CONTRACTOR URBAN SPLASH PROJECTS
COST £14.8 MILLION
PHOTOGRAPHER CHRIS BRINK

URBIS
.MANCHESTER .IAN SIMPSON ARCHITECTS

Urbis is Manchester's major Millennium Commission-funded cultural project and fulfils the city's desire for a landmark project to arise from the ashes of the destruction wrought by the IRA in 1996. An international competition led to the appointment of Ian Simpson, whose sculptural building houses a uniquely flexible museum that tells the story not just of Manchester, but of world cities. The triple-glazed skin not only provides a constantly changing surface but also forms a buffer zone, ventilated top and bottom to dissipate solar gain. The building is roofed with prepatinated copper tiles whose scale relates to the glass of the façade.

This unprecedented example of the museum type has been housed in a dramatic and distinctively shaped building whose semi-translucent glass sheath gives it externally a curious scaleless quality. It is intimately linked to nearby beautifully designed landscaping. Together they form part of the major inner-city transformation of the environs of Manchester Cathedral.

To a degree, the building is a spectacular one-liner, a one-sided ziggurat of progressively shorter floors set in a single space under a single roof; the drama of the idea emphasized by the highly unusual use of a funicular lift – a moving viewing platform rising above the city and a visitor attraction in its own right. The service wall obliterates any view to the nearby street but an impression of the surrounding city is had everywhere else through the fritted glass, as if through a veil. Only at the very top in the spectacular restaurant does the building again reconnect to the city.

The exhibits (by others) have their own agenda but the vertical subdivision gives the visitor both a sense of the organisation of the whole and a psychological breathing space between the different parts of this very exhausting and full exhibition.

MANCHESTER CITY COUNCIL SHORTLISTED FOR THE RIBA CLIENT OF THE YEAR

CLIENT MANCHESTER CITY COUNCIL
STRUCTURAL ENGINEER MARTIN STOCKLEY ASSOCIATES
SERVICES ENGINEER ROBERTS AND PARTNERS
QS DAVIS LANGDON & EVEREST
CONTRACTOR LAING
COST £25 MILLION
PHOTOGRAPHER PHOTEC

GROUND-FLOOR PLAN

101 .NORTH-WEST

WAULK MILL
.MANCHESTER .TOTAL ARCHITECTURE

This project, a paradigm of reuse and conservation, involved two adjacent mill buildings, part of the Murray's Mills complex of 1842. This, Manchester's oldest surviving group of mills, stands in Ancoats, an area shortlisted for World Heritage Site status as the world's first industrial suburb. The brief was to create self-contained office accommodation with an entrance and common areas that would reflect the design aspirations of potential media and design clients. The buildings' listing necessitated continuous and close collaboration with English Heritage, whose requirements were often at odds with the commercial needs of the client. The success of the scheme lies in the balance struck between the two.

The project is in the vanguard of the redevelopment of Ancoats (it is a brave economic beacon in an area of dereliction). The same client has been appointed lead developer for the Manchester Millennium Village and the sensitive redevelopment of Waulk Mill will serve as a benchmark for further projects currently in the planning stages.

The office functions have been accommodated without fuss into the old mills and here much of the original fabric is revealed to good effect. However, foyer, toilets and lift have been housed in a spectacular new space formed by the removal of all the floors in one structural bay, as well as making a dramatic entrance. This move reveals the reality of the construction of the building in a didactic manner and focuses attention on the wonderful original spiral staircase. Externally, the work is well detailed but unfussy and again will set a benchmark for adjacent developments.

CLIENT URBAN SPLASH
STRUCTURAL ENGINEER URBAN SPLASH
LANDSCAPE ARCHITECT LANDSCAPE PROJECTS
QS SIMON FENTON PARTNERSHIP
CONTRACTOR URBAN SPLASH PROJECTS
COST £2.7 MILLION
PHOTOGRAPHER RICHARD COOPER – PHOTOFLEX

3

MILLENNIUM GALLERIES AND WINTER GARDEN .SHEFFIELD .PRINGLE RICHARDS SHARRATT

The Winter Garden is the largest city-centre botanical garden in Britain and the associated galleries are among the most flexible venues for travelling exhibitions outside London. The two parts of the project are strikingly different. The huge glasshouse has a powerful, almost animal quality – a giant ribcage – yet makes direct reference to trees in the massive glue-laminated timber parabolic arches. The heavy aroma of damp earth and lush vegetation is almost shocking in the noisy, hard-edged, fumed-filled centre of Sheffield.

By contrast, the galleries are cool, calm and precise, a carefully controlled essay in heavyweight prefabrication. 'The Avenue' is a sequence of tall and generous spaces with a remarkably light, relaxed quality. It runs the full length of the building, serving as a public foyer, an orientation space for the galleries, and a link between the Winter Garden and Sheffield Hallam University to the east.

In the galleries themselves the architects have achieved a difficult balance between spaces of strong architectural character and a very high level of adaptability. These rooms could have been rather dull – constant height, insistent grid to accommodate variable display layouts and neutral colours – but controlled top-lighting, high-quality materials and restrained but robust detailing combine to create a flexible space with a sense of occasion. It may prove a difficult space for curators but the flexibility does offer the possibility of a wide variety of artistic experience.

But the real strength of these buildings is as urban design. There is an intriguing ambiguity in their spatial qualities – are they indoors or outdoors, routes or destinations? It is very much a case of both/and rather than either/or. As the architects note, these are not so much 'objects in an open city square, but streets and spaces mined out of a dense bit of urban fabric … new routes that lead to other destinations, linking three city squares'.

CLIENT SHEFFIELD CITY COUNCIL
STRUCTURAL ENGINEER BURO HAPPOLD
SERVICES ENGINEER BURO HAPPOLD
LANDSCAPE ARCHITECT WEDDLE LANDSCAPE DESIGN
QS SHEFFIELD DESIGN & PROPERTY
CONTRACTOR INTERSERVE PROJECT SERVICES LTD
COST £17.5 MILLION
PHOTOGRAPHER MARTINE HAMILTON KNIGHT

PRIVATE HOUSE
.WETHERBY .OMI ARCHITECTS

This is a rich and subtle piece of architecture and a wonderfully relaxed place to live. The starting point was a modest Georgian house on a stunning riverside site with glorious southerly exposure. The existing building is respected but transformed by careful surgery to its upper floors and basement and an expansive, luxurious extension at the level of the original ground-floor.

The overall conception is brilliantly simple; the detailed resolution satisfyingly complex. The extension is a composition of layered planes, a subtle, knowing contrast to the 'architecture of rooms' of the original house. The extension grows effortlessly from the existing floor plan to create a series of highly controlled but delightfully comfortable living spaces. Views are exploited to the full, but do not dominate the interior.

The detailed design is immaculate – sliding screens that move at the touch of a finger, an internal window that reveals the distant view, a simple skylight that washes the end wall with light, minimal detailing that is elegant but robust. The range of materials is small but well-chosen to complement the gentle golden stone and white paint of the original – limestone, untreated oak, self-coloured render, grey-painted steel.

Despite the steep fall across the site, the house connects effortlessly with the terraced garden that steps down in a series of stone, timber and grassed terraces to the river.

This is a beautifully conceived and immaculately constructed home that integrates old and new and responds thoughtfully to its setting.

CLIENT PRIVATE
STRUCTURAL ENGINEER WOOLGAR HUNTER
QS HARVEY & CO
CONTRACTORS MAYSAND / CAREY &
GREENSLADE / COMPASS
COST £600,000
PHOTOGRAPHER DENNIS GILBERT – VIEW

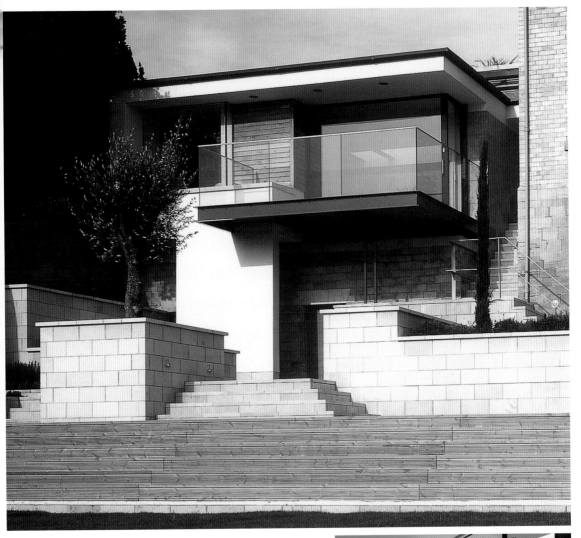

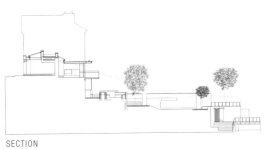

SECTION

107 .YORKSHIRE

WHITBY ABBEY VISITOR CENTRE
.WHITBY .STANTON WILLIAMS

This is an exemplary project that demonstrates how finely judged contemporary design can not only fit comfortably into a historic context, but can also lift it to a completely new level. Whitby Abbey is an extraordinarily evocative ruin, silhouetted on a rocky headland dominating the town. It is the most sensitive of sites – a scheduled ancient monument in a conservation area, next to a Grade I-listed house. The client, English Heritage, carried the project through with real vision – this could so easily have been a timid medieval pastiche or a 'look at me' stand-alone pavilion.

This imaginative intervention, informed by detailed archaeological investigation, reinhabits the long-abandoned shell of a 17th-century house. Early in the last century its windows were bricked up and generations of visitors experienced it as an empty volume unconnected with the setting and uncommunicative of the turbulent history of the site.

The insertions are very simple. Two floors of interpretative displays linked by a straight staircase, a lift, a glass and timber screen on the south face – where a large section of wall had disappeared – and an almost invisible flat roof, have been dropped into the existing enclosure. There is no doubt about what is old and what is new. Old work has been stabilized; new construction barely touches it. The windows, for example, have been reopened, reconnecting the building with the newly excavated forecourt, but they have been designed to have minimal impact on surrounding stonework. All the new work is in a precise modern style, simple, direct and functional – and it is beautifully made, using a restrained palette of the best materials. No-one seeing this building could believe that craftsmanship is dead in England.

It is a truly accessible building. Designed with those with disabilities in mind, it also gives access to parts of the site that were inaccessible to wheelchair users and those unable to negotiate steps.

SHORTLISTED FOR THE ADAPT TRUST ACCESS AWARD AND THE CROWN ESTATE CONSERVATION AWARD

CLIENT ENGLISH HERITAGE
STRUCTURAL ENGINEERS STEVENSON CALAM ASSOCIATES / DEWHURST MACFARLANE & PARTNERS
SERVICES ENGINEER ENGLISH HERITAGE SERVICES
QS CITEX BUCKNALL AUSTIN
INTERPRETATION PAST FORWARD
ACCESS CONSULTANT PMT
CONTRACTOR WILLIAM BIRCH & SONS LTD
COST £5.36 MILLION
PHOTOGRAPHER MARTINE HAMILTON KNIGHT

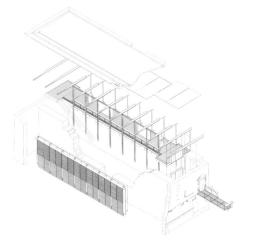

YORKSHIRE SCULPTURE PARK ENTRANCE BUILDING
.WEST BRETTON .FEILDEN CLEGG BRADLEY

On paper this building seems strangely incomplete. The plans show a takeaway coffee bar, a gift shop, toilets, a café on the upper floor, some meeting rooms and an enormous foyer. There are no galleries, no interactive displays, no interpretative installations. A visit to the Sculpture Park resolves this paradox at once – the building seems exactly right in scale and programme. It is described as a visitor centre but is better understood as the front-of-house of a giant theatre of sculpture that spreads across hundreds of hectares of gorgeous Yorkshire countryside.

The architects cite the Burrell Collection and the Louisiana Museum as precedents. Like them, it is intimately connected to its site. An essentially linear composition extends the geometry of the formal terrace, part of the 18th-century landscape design, into the park. The visitor is drawn from the car park to a line of trees and on to a rusting steel path (that is progressively being incised with the names of the sculpture park's supporters). There can be no doubt where to go. You are led straight through the entrance into a spacious concourse. To the right an elegant sandstone colonnade gives access to meeting rooms, toilets and offices in an adjacent building. To the left is the landscape – from trees that seem almost within reach to distant views – seen first through the shop and a little further on through a beautifully detailed glass wall. The concourse passes over the 18th-century ha-ha that the plan gently accommodates by a slight adjustment to its geometry. At the far end the visitor emerges into the park and on to the site of the next phase of the composition, a series of galleries that will merge with the landscape.

This is a very assured work that admirably fulfils its function as the entrance to an extraordinary sculpture collection. It is an appropriately sculptural work of architecture that delights with a relaxed sequence of spatial experiences, careful orchestration of views, thoughtful use of materials and a real sense of craftsmanship in its detailing and construction.

CLIENT YORKSHIRE SCULPTURE PARK
STRUCTURAL ENGINEER MICHAEL HEAL ASSOCIATES
SERVICES ENGINEER ID BUILDING SERVICES
LANDSCAPE ARCHITECT LAND USE CONSULTANTS
QS BURNLEY WILSON FISH
CONTRACTOR GALLIFORD NORTHERN
COST £3.9 MILLION
PHOTOGRAPHER PETER COOK – VIEW

MOAT HOUSE
.DORSINGTON .GLENN HOWELLS ARCHITECTS

A glazed room is attached to an old manor house, and cantilevers out over the water-filled moat that surrounds it. The house is a rambling conglomeration dating back to the 12th century and exhibits all the virtues we would expect in such a historic building. It also exhibits the standard drawbacks, including low ceilings, even lower beams, and small windows, with consequent gloomy interiors.

The Miesian glass box is a familiar architectural type. While its iconic status can, sometimes, encourage its use for purely formal reasons, here it is successful because it is so appropriate to its brief and location. The glass box complements the old house in as happy a way as is possible. Stepping into it from the house engenders a wonderful feeling of release and relief, giving the whole house balance – light and shade. The release comes from engagement with the wider landscape and is followed, as you move into the space, with specific engagement with the water below. Slide open one of the big glass panels and the whole outside world rushes in – air, wind, smells, birds singing and water flowing, the simple room now becoming a catwalk, terrace, pool room, rocky outcrop or diving board.

The judges particularly enjoyed the way that such a small, simple space effectively delivers a rich sequence of sensory experiences. The more standard architectural response to a Miesian box is to examine its detailing, and comment on the honing and simplicity of layout, material and junction. The judges found no fault with the architect's response.

A little room full of intense, sensory enjoyment, demonstrating the power of architecture to transform all round it, it is much used and loved by the family who commissioned it.

SHORTLISTED FOR THE STEPHEN LAWRENCE PRIZE

CLIENTS IGOR AND MARION KOLODOTSCHKO
STRUCTURAL ENGINEER HASKINS ROBINSON WATERS
CONTRACTOR COLOR ESTATES
COST £97,000
PHOTOGRAPHER ROD DORLING

THE CENTRE FOR MATHEMATICAL SCIENCES, UNIVERSITY OF CAMBRIDGE
.CAMBRIDGE .EDWARD CULLINAN ARCHITECTS

The centre houses the University of Cambridge Faculty of Maths, which is composed of the Department of Applied Maths and Theoretical Physics and the Department of Pure Maths and Maths with Statistics. Lying in a conservation area characterized by high-quality 1930/40s residential architecture, the challenge was to accommodate a large building on the site in a way that was in sympathy with its domestic neighbours.

In order to address the issues of bulk and massing, the building has been organized into seven pavilions housing offices, lecture theatres and research laboratories. The buildings are placed in a symmetrical order around a central axis, in front of which sits the gatehouse and library (containing the Stephen Hawking Archive). The central core, housing the larger public spaces such as lecture halls, has a grass roof that serves as a garden. The client had requested a workplace conducive to a variety of working methods, from quiet contemplative thought in individual offices to thought-provoking exchanges between large groups in communal areas; this arrangement seems to work well. The pavilions are composed in a similar way to the surrounding domestic buildings, with front doors at ground level, a lobby and a central core around which the social and public heart of the building functions.

This is architecture of great force and ambition. It is a masterful exercise of coherent vision, a grand building – in scale and in geometry. It evokes its purpose of housing the mathematical minds of the University of Cambridge and has gravitas. It is also circumspect in its regard for its neighbours – evident with its deceptive (and skilful) concealment of its bulk, its domestic language, its landscaping, and its energy policy.

The brief also requested a comfortable environment with low energy usage. The burial of the building and the heaviness of its roof are used to cool it as well as to minimize its mass.

CLIENT EMBS, UNIVERSITY OF CAMBRIDGE
STRUCTURAL ENGINEER BURO HAPPOLD
SERVICES ENGINEER ROGER PRESTON & PARTNERS
LANDSCAPE ARCHITECT LIVINGSTON EYRE ASSOCIATES
QS NORTHCROFTS
PROJECT MANAGER DAVIS LANGDON & EVEREST
CONTRACTOR LAING/ROBERT MCALPINE
COST £50 MILLION
PHOTOGRAPHER MANDY REYNOLDS – FOTOFORUM (TOP); DILL FAULKES (BOTTOM RIGHT)

SHORTLISTED FOR THE RIBA JOURNAL SUSTAINABILITY AWARD
UNIVERSITY OF CAMBRIDGE SHORTLISTED FOR THE RIBA CLIENT OF THE YEAR

LOWESTOFT WASTE WATER WORKS
.LOWESTOFT .BARBER CASANOVAS RUFFLES

Anglian Water Services commissioned a £76 million plant to treat a large volume of sewage and waste water in a way that would minimize impact on its environment. The plant is enormous; the solution was to cover it with a domed structure 160 metres long by 130 metres wide.

The choice of the elliptical roof structure is ingenious and by rationalising the geometry the architects have made it cost-effective This is a brilliant concept – a shallow dome on a hilltop reminiscent of a stone-age fort. The building is mostly below ground, contained within a 7.5-metre-high retaining wall. Only a 1.5-metre section under the eaves is visible.

It is the first building of its kind. Such plants were previously situated on open greenfield sites, with smells blowing out in all directions. This one sets a precedent: safe, clean and low in impact on the environment. The design also produces a safe, even pleasant working environment. Natural light permeates the dome via eight 9-metre-diameter double-glazed roof lights. A special light-diffusing glass has been used to minimize the impact of sunlight.

This must be recognized as a significant piece of architecture, fit for its purpose, related to its context, appropriate in its structural and servicing systems and beautifully and unobtrusively detailed. Most remarkable of all, the thing works so well that the entire process is operated by just one man.

SHORTLISTED FOR THE RIBA JOURNAL SUSTAINABILITY AWARD

CLIENT ANGLIAN WATER SERVICES LTD
STRUCTURAL ENGINEER ANTHONY HUNT ASSOCIATES
LANDSCAPE ARCHITECT LANDSCAPE DESIGN ASSOCIATES
QS FAITHFUL & GOULD
CONTRACTOR JOHN MOWLEM
COST £76 MILLION, INCLUDING INFRASTRUCTURE
PHOTOGRAPHER TIMOTHY SOAR

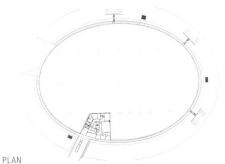

PLAN

THE PAVILION, NEW MALTINGS
.NAYLAND .KNOX BHAVAN ARCHITECTS

The Pavilion is the latest addition to a fine architectural tradition on this site. The main house by Edward Cullinan dates from the 1960s and was extensively remodelled by Penoyre and Prasad in the 1980s. Simon Knox worked on both schemes, so the clients were more than happy to appoint him to solve their problem: too few bedrooms for a large family. His solution was a freestanding pavilion housing two bedrooms, a bathroom and kitchen, using matching materials. The structure, though in the spirit of the original, is not a facsimile but a new interpretation.

Preservation of a mature beech hedge to protect the pathway and the main garden was the primary intention of the brief. The roofline has been drawn with the sense of harmony in mind. The client wished to maintain a distinction between the pavilion and the main house although they were to read as a unified group. This has been achieved.

In remodelling the house, Penoyre and Prasad opened it out into a series of open-ended living spaces, cleverly reinterpreting the house. They made much of the different levels with the space and the result is light and fun. The most recent addition is on one level. It is more manicured and elegant but just as playful, experimenting with different woods and colourful finishes (as in the red bathrooms). The details of the original building are echoed rather than copied – there is a sense of evolution rather than conservation.

The inhabitants enjoy an all-round view of their garden and the surrounding landscape. It is a complex of living buildings that does not hide itself but blends with the environment, engaging with the context rather than being passively compliant to it.

SHORTLISTED FOR THE MANSER MEDAL

CLIENT PRIVATE
STRUCTURAL ENGINEER JOHN ROMER
QS ERIC COWELL
CONTRACTOR CUBITT THEOBALD LTD
COST £303,000
PHOTOGRAPHER DENNIS GILBERT – VIEW

POSTGRADUATE HOUSING, CHURCHILL COLLEGE .CAMBRIDGE .COTTRELL & VERMEULEN

The college commissioned accommodation for 30 postgraduates on a former garden site between an arts-and-crafts house and a 1970s residential block. The architects won the competition by proposing a group of three buildings within an orchard garden. Other competitors had proposed a single block.

In a conservation area and surrounded by sensitive and vocal neighbours, the architects had a stiff challenge to design something that would be acceptable in the context without resorting to pastiche. They have succeeded admirably.

Each block houses ten postgraduate students new to the college and the country. All the rooms are wrapped around a circulation core – each block is rotated and flipped to take in the best views and respond to its specific location. Each has double aspects facing out to the orchard garden. The internal planning allows an area for study and an area for resting or sleeping. The design strategy works well from the inside out with proportions dictated by a tight floor-to-ceiling height and stairwell bay windows. The skill of the design lies in the fusion of different internal and external spatial needs.

Undoubtedly the most striking move was in taking its cue from the arts-and-crafts building in its heavy-feeling hand-made clay tiles. The architects wrapped their internally organized building in the same material and gave the same emphasis to roof and wall. On a secondary level, the use of materials then followed their contextual understanding of the site – concrete cladding panels refer to Sheppard Robson's college buildings – the tiles sweep over and around the new residences in a similar fashion to the adjacent Baillie Scott house. The tiles feature a motif of silicon molecules (the research work of a student), giving a neat geometric representation of the nature of the arts and crafts tradition.

The garden design was central to the project and was developed in close collaboration with the college gardener.

CLIENT CHURCHILL COLLEGE
STRUCTURAL ENGINEER BURO HAPPOLD
SERVICES ENGINEER MAX FORDHAM &
PARTNERS
QS DAVID LANGDON & EVEREST
LANDSCAPE ARCHITECT JOHN MOORE
CONTRACTOR C G FRANKLIN
COST £1.65 MILLION
PHOTOGRAPHER PETER GRANT

SHANKS MILLENNIUM BRIDGE
.PETERBOROUGH .WHITBYBIRD BRIDGES TEAM

The bridge across the River Nene is the final link in Peterborough's Green Wheel Millennium Project, providing a pedestrian and cycle route encircling the city. The client, chief executive of the Peterborough Environment City Trust, initiated the architectural competition, wrote the design brief, prepared the environmental impact assessment and raised the funding. His vision set the scene for an exemplary piece of design that is at once integrated into its modern fen landscape, yet echoes the historical significance of the site. It gives an exhilarating experience to cyclists, pedestrians and horse riders without compromising on biodiversity. It is now recognized and loved as a local landmark.

The design ingeniously combines the different needs of bridge users with the natural lie of the land. The concentric curves are the direct product of the existing site levels. The Corten steel material was perceptively chosen as an elemental one that weathers and becomes part of the particular natural and industrial landscape.

The structural articulation is inspired and subtle, placing the prosaic into the realm of the poetic. The main structural element, conceived as a pair of 'folded arms', offers the cantilevered pedestrian walkway on the inner rim of the curve, while the Corten box forms the bridgeway and the structural spine. The pedestrian deck is raised above the bridgeway, visually reducing the overall structural mass of the bridge. A further level of subtlety evolves from the need to shield users from the wind and prevent silhouetting against the skyline, which was expected to disturb the river birds. The difference in level creates two scales within one supple structure. It also gives each user a prime sense of place. The vertical elements (balustrades and support ribs) resonate with the surrounding landscape of grass and riverbed reeds and the dynamic flow of the curve makes the viewer almost expect that the bridge will blow with the wind. (It doesn't!)

CLIENT PETERBOROUGH ENVIRONMENT CITY TRUST
STRUCTURAL ENGINEER WHITBYBIRD
QS POSFORD HASKONING
CONTRACTOR MAY GURNEY
COST £800,000
PHOTOGRAPHER RICHARD BRYANT – ARCAID

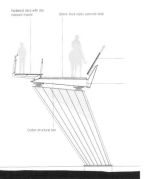

Hardwood deck with slip resistant inserts

90mm thick insitu concrete deck

Corten structural box

SECTION

SUTTON HOO VISITOR CENTRE
.WOODBRIDGE .VAN HEYNINGEN & HAWARD
ARCHITECTS

This National Trust Visitor Centre was initiated to protect the burial ground, to care for and conserve the surrounding landscape and to increase the public's enjoyment of the site and its understanding of Anglo-Saxon England by the creation of buildings that are sympathetic to the subject. The brief also called for a scheme that would provide good accessibility to visitors of all abilities, that would be an exemplar of good environmental practice, and that would require minimal maintenance and therefore low running costs.

The architects saw the project as needing to identify quintessentially 'Sutton Hoo' qualities and to embody them into the nature of the building – and to incorporate good environmental practice. To preserve the serenity of the burial ground the new buildings were located at a distance and orientated to minimize visual impact by falling into the lie of the land.

Barn-type structures were chosen, due to their familiarity in rural settings. Materials and construction systems involve state-of-the-art minimum-environmental-impact practices: timber; low embodied energy; natural daylighting through rooflights; deep overhangs for solar protection and glare reduction while allowing winter sun penetration; stack effect reducing the need for air-conditioning; rainwater for toilets; natural insulation (recycled newspaper) in 'breathing wall' construction; and acoustically pleasant spaces achieved through sound-absorbing materials concealed in the ceiling.

This is a consummately high-quality piece of architecture. The design of the spaces themselves follows through the architects' noble environmental ideals of practice into beautifully light, elegant and calming spaces. It is an innovative and subtle assembly of buildings – reading from the past and projecting positively into the future. An utterly coherent design.

CLIENTS NATIONAL TRUST / SUTTON HOO VISITOR CENTRE
STRUCTURAL ENGINEER PRICE & MYERS
SERVICES ENGINEER MAX FORDHAM & PARTNERS
QS DAVIS LANGDON & EVEREST
CONTRACTOR HAYMILLS (CONTRACTORS) LTD
COST £3.7 MILLION
PHOTOGRAPHER HEINI SCHNEEBELI

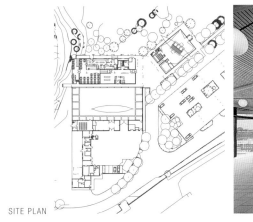

SITE PLAN

VICTORIA STREET
.CAMBRIDGE .5TH STUDIO LTD

From a modest low-budget brief, the architects have transformed a tiny terraced house into a seminal piece of architecture. They have also transformed the life of its owner.

The terraced site is long and narrow. A 1960s extension to the Victorian house had cut it off from the garden. The client suffers from ME, which requires long periods of confinement; the setting of the house is crucial. She asked that her house become easier to navigate, have more light and spaciousness and more visual contact with the outside in order to minimize her sense of isolation from the outside world during these periods. The technique has involved the combination of cleverly organized plans and sections. The art has been in allowing her to feel the outside by giving her a continuously changing sense of external light.

The architects should be highly commended for the intelligence and sensitivity of their solution. In addition to a remodelled place of repositioned bedrooms and bathrooms and the removal of central walls, they have fundamentally challenged domestic renovation by the use of a cleverly manipulated section. Rooflights are placed to give natural light into all of the rooms and the insertion of a structurally glazed first-floor landing, conveniently placed mirrors, a structurally glazed kitchen exterior, and a glazed central gutter, all carry the ever-changing outside light into all parts of the house.

The experience of forming a rich piece of modernism on a shoestring budget, employing the skills of a local builder unused to working with structural glass, was a challenge to which all involved have risen admirably. The result is one highly delighted client.

CLIENT PRIVATE
STRUCTURAL ENGINEER HARRIS & SUTHERLAND
CONTRACTOR ALDER & ANDREWS
COST £40,000
PHOTOGRAPHER PAUL SMOOTHY

NATIONAL MARITIME MUSEUM CORNWALL
.FALMOUTH .LONG & KENTISH

Like Venice, the only way to approach Falmouth is from the sea. The sea approach identifies the museum as a key point of reference along the waterside. It sits in its context as if it had always been there: silvering material, shimmering in sunshine, mystic in grey light, tower and rising boatshed as counterpoint forms, quietly indicating its public nature and true date of origin. The approach from the town has the prospect of the strong south gable, oak battens woven into simple threads, accentuating the drifting forms, with the entrance the primary opening that no one can mistake.

You start in the Dark Gallery with a showcase of miniature boats like an aquarium of vessels, and finish in the Observatory Tower, overlooking the panorama of maritime Falmouth. Hall spaces with flotillas of boats and spectacular audio-visual presentations are interwoven for the visitor via observation perches on the ramping wooden path, like stopping points on a corniche. The use of wood beautifully holds the exterior and interior forms together, with differing grains to give identity to different spaces. The spatial sequence, use of materials, organisation of activity spaces and setting of the exhibits result in a complete and continuous environment for the user, enjoyable, educational and stimulating for all ages. Inside and outside are periodically linked via glimpses or extended views of café and observatory. Physical connections also link the interior with waterborne exhibits on pontoons in the harbour.

The building is rich throughout; full of scenic event, it still feels continuous. It demonstrates architecture at its very best in its relationship to the town and to the people who will use it, visit it and work in it.

CLIENT NATIONAL MARITIME MUSEUM
STRUCTURAL ENGINEER ARUP
SERVICES ENGINEER ARUP
EXHIBITION DESIGN LAND DESIGN STUDIO
QS DAVIS LANGDON & EVEREST
CONTRACTORS ALFRED MCALPINE / INTERSERVE LTD
COST £15.35 MILLION (BUILDING) / £4.25 MILLION (EXHIBITION)
PHOTOGRAPHER PETER DURRANT

SITE PLAN

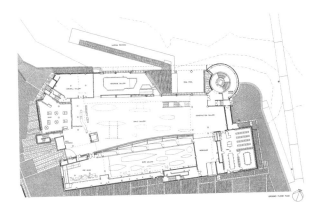

CHAPA
.MALMESBURY .A-EM

This is a townhouse that rejects the fashionable or pastiche and creates a charming and loving relationship between those who live here and the town they live in. This is convivial, charming and – most of all – loving architecture.

Set on a small and awkward industrial site in a terraced street, the design borrows from southern European planning to create an innovative sequence of living spaces for the resident who required particular attention to be paid to accessibility.

A covered L-shaped courtyard provides room for a car and a welcome to guests. The space receives daylight from an internal lightwell and, intriguingly, you are enclosed by the stone walls of the surrounding buildings, including a gothic nunnery.

Across the courtyard, the entrance hall is signalled by the iroko wood that embraces all the inhabited spaces. A spiral stair enclosed in a bright yellow tabernacle-like shaft rises to the living level. To one side is a wheelchair platform. Arriving at the living level, you see the remarkable use of space. Living area, dining area and open-plan kitchen inventively use the L-shape, terminating in two terraces and light sources, one looking over the pavement and down the winding street, the other within the white-walled enclosure of the nunnery. Bedrooms and bathrooms are organized landside of the living space with the master bedroom enjoying the light and prospect of the lightwell and the second bedroom a sky-window and sky-vent.

The living space has a comfortable, convivial yet inventive and highly architectural character with soothing lighting at all times.

CLIENT PRIVATE
STRUCTURAL ENGINEER ELLIOTT WOOD PARTNERSHIP
SERVICES ENGINEER MAX FORDHAM ASSOCIATES
QS JENKINS HANSFORD PARTNERSHIP
CONTRACTOR A C NURDEN LTD
COST £300,000
PHOTOGRAPHER ALAN WILLIAMS

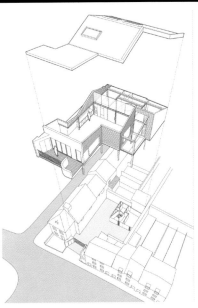

COWLEY MANOR HOTEL AND SPA
.CHELTENHAM .DE MATOS STOREY RYAN

The brief called for a distinctive 30-bedroom hotel and spa that combined the seemingly incompatible English country-house style with contemporary living; the architects have succeeded in pulling it off. The house, most recently used as a nursing home, has been simply restored and made the main hotel: the stables are now additional bedrooms and the grounds the setting for an elegant modern spa building. The new buildings and interiors work in harmonious discord with the historic house and parkland. The choice of materials, furniture and lighting result in a complete piece of work. Each bedroom and bathroom is individually composed. Wardrobes are concealed like priests' holes behind the renovated oak panelling that fully lines the bedrooms.

Spatial character, materials and colour interventions are used throughout to reinvent the period pieces. The design is full of event, interlinking historic and new, with entertaining cedar shingle lavatories under a domed glazed ceiling at the heart of the ground floor. Art, textiles and furniture enrich the public and residential guestrooms. By day the project appears to have been designed for daylight, but in the evening a therapeutic closing down produces an equally convivial night-time setting.

The new spa is set away from the main house and pushed down behind a grassed mound, topped with a carpet of lavender and surrounded by mature trees so as to be hidden from visitors as they arrive. The setting of the spa transforms the historic trio of house, stables and former estate church into a 21st-century quartet. The pools are beautiful, inside and out, seamless with the landscape, reflecting, relaxing, and visually exhilarating. Guests can lie back and look up at the sky.

This reinvention for 21st-century life is an exemplar of the way that our historic buildings and landscapes can be sustained.

SHORTLISTED FOR THE ARCHITECTS' JOURNAL FIRST BUILDING AWARD AND THE CROWN ESTATE CONSERVATION AWARD

CLIENTS JESSICA SAINSBURY AND PETER FRANKOPAN
STRUCTURAL ENGINEER PRICE & MYERS
CONTRACTOR PETTIFER CONSTRUCTION
COST UNDISCLOSED
PHOTOGRAPHER DAVID GRANDORGE

NEW HOUSE ON EVENING HILL .POOLE HARBOUR .HORDEN CHERRY LEE ARCHITECTS

It took six years for the architect to win planning permission for this house overlooking Poole Harbour, but it was worth the wait. It is a consistent part of a long Horden tradition. His first building, Courtyard House, also in Poole, dates from his student days of 1969 (though executed three years later); the Yacht House in the New Forest was done in 1982; the Poole Study Gallery is from 2000: all explored glass-and-steel construction in a site-specific way.

This is the latest manifestation of a simple idea that is so hard to implement elegantly. If you can only design a house as high as a fence, then this is the way to do it. On arriving through the white garden wall, the showcase living space acts as a magnifying glass to the panoramic view of the seascape and island beyond. A grassed courtyard enclosed by house and fence forms an external living room with sun and shade, but sheltered from sea breezes. The flat steel lid of a roof accentuates the panoramic shot. It is all very Hockney, without the pool – that is still to come. The floor of the house extends the courtyard to reveal a double-height space. Rooms above and below accentuate that view.

The house is a like a piece of origami, a white paper building with void and balcony folded into one: a single-storey aspect on the north side, and a double storey on the sea side. A glazed walkway links the glazed bedrooms with the double-height space to the living area.

CLIENT PRIVATE
STRUCTURAL ENGINEERS ANTHONY HUNT ASSOCIATES / B E WILLIS
QS DENLEY KING PARTNERSHIP
CONTRACTOR DELTA DESIGN AND BUILD
COST UNDISCLOSED
PHOTOGRAPHER DENNIS GILBERT – VIEW

135 .WESSEX

OXSTALLS CAMPUS, UNIVERSITY OF GLOUCESTERSHIRE
.GLOUCESTER .FEILDEN CLEGG BRADLEY

This mini campus shows that it is important not only to create a masterplan for large groups of buildings but also to follow this route for small groupings. The Learning Resource Centre, Sports Science Centre and residential building are inter-related within a suburban site of mature trees to create a simple and successful living and learning environment.

The east side of the central outside space is lined with student accommodation and the Students' Union. The housing is in simple cubic terraced groups and finished in two-tone render and silvering oak boards. On the other side of the space is the multi-level Learning Resource Centre. Vertical circulation is via a grand staircase, with the galleried floors for electronic learning enjoying a fully glazed north light. A double-height glazed colonnade links the visitor to the sports science and administration building. The link is given an Oxbridge feel by crossing a rectangular body of water that runs from the central space out to the tree-lined edge, visually connecting the movement of students and staff with passers-by in the locality – a sort of visual outreach. The café faces the sunlight, accentuated by the reflecting pool of water, and enjoys a wooden decked terrace. The Sports Science Centre uses a similar language, with render, oak boards and glazing relating well to the bigger box-like building forms.

Energy use and life cycle costs are close to the university's heart, for ethical reasons as well as responsible management. Early energy-consumption figures are pleasingly low and the introduction of photovoltaics should reduce them still further. The architect and client team have got it just about right in all respects.

CLIENT UNIVERSITY OF GLOUCESTERSHIRE
STRUCTURAL ENGINEER WHITBYBIRD
PROJECT MANAGER AND QS BURNLEY WILSON FISH
CONTRACTOR HBG CONSTRUCTION
COST £9.5 MILLION
PHOTOGRAPHER MANDY REYNOLDS – FOTOFORUM

137 .WESSEX

CHIPPING NORTON SPORTS CENTRE
.CHIPPING NORTON .FEILDEN CLEGG BRADLEY

This sport and leisure centre is on a prominent edge-of-town site serving a nearby school as well as the community. It contains a four-court sports hall, a 25-metre swimming pool, a fitness suite, dance studio and squash courts, as well as changing rooms and social areas. The housing of all these facilities is handled with skill and economy, in particular the daylighting of the pool and the sports hall, where the computer and physical modelling undertaken at design stage has paid off handsomely in producing glare-free, beautifully naturally lit spaces. There is an atmosphere of calmness and light, of health and well-being. In particular it is in the circulation areas that the architects' care and attention can be readily seen. They are flooded with daylight and they focus on views. In the reception-cum-social area, simple Scandinavian-style circular stools and tables sit under a huge circular rooflight with an orange kerb. All wall finishes are white, giving a slightly austere character that seems entirely appropriate to the healthy activities the spaces contain.

The layout of the scheme is deceptively simple: flat-roofed blocks in plain narrow brickwork flank a long roof-lit corridor. The brickwork is relieved by large glazed openings and a glulam timber-structured pool hall. A simply designed car park and forecourt leading to the entrance are totally integrated into the design of the building. The choice of architectural form, construction and materials, fittings, furniture, finishes and planting is judicious and restrained. The architects have been concerned to produce an economical and sustainable design appropriate for both the community and the school.

CLIENT WEST OXFORDSHIRE DISTRICT COUNCIL
STRUCTURAL ENGINEER WHITBYBIRD
SERVICES ENGINEER BKN ASSOCIATES
QS BOXALL SAYER
CONTRACTOR HINKINS & FREWIN
COST £4 MILLION
PHOTOGRAPHER ANDREW SOUTHALL

ERCOL FACTORY
.PRINCES RISBOROUGH .HORDEN CHERRY LEE ARCHITECTS

A new building on a brownfield site, once the home of the Building Research Station, houses the family-owned furniture-manufacturing company Ercol. It previously occupied three separate buildings 11 kilometres away at High Wycombe. Here the making of furniture has been rationalized within an exemplary sustainable framework, giving the relocated workforce a pleasurable and stimulating environment.

The building is composed with thought and restraint and is laid out with a splendid clarity. From a long, low, simply clad grey block, a carefully detailed white steel frame emerges in a series of layers that reach out to enclose existing woodland and an elegant glass showroom, offices and restaurant. Within, lofty office spaces and showroom are suffused with daylight. A window wall to the open-plan production areas gives a dramatic background view of trees to the manufacturing activities.

The sustainable strategy for the project has been exemplary. Materials from the existing buildings were recycled on this brownfield site, which is within walking distance of the railway station. Furniture manufacturing is a notoriously noisy and dusty activity, but here acoustic treatment has reduced the acoustic energy escaping to 2.5 per cent of that of standard factory construction. Electric load is half that of the old factory. All dust and waste wood is stored and recycled or burnt to minimize fossil-fuel use.

The client, managing director Edward Tadros, is the third generation of the Ercol family in the firm. Together, he and his architects have produced an enormously enjoyable and practical building that has helped to develop a closer sense of community between factory and office workers, while Ercol customers can now see how the furniture is assembled and made, and view the finished products in well laid-out display settings.

CLIENT EDWARD TADROS, ERCOL FURNITURE LTD
STRUCTURAL ENGINEER WSP SOUTH LTD
SERVICES ENGINEER CUNDALL JOHNSON & PARTNERS
QS AYH PLC
CONTRACTOR MARBANK CONSTRUCTION LTD
COST £12 MILLION
PHOTOGRAPHER DENNIS GILBERT – VIEW

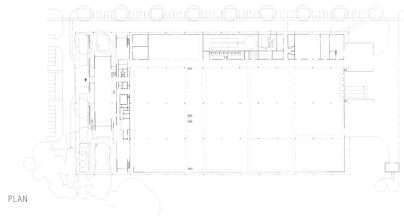

PLAN

141 .SOUTH

INEOS HEADQUARTERS
.LYNDHURST .ARCHITECTURE PLB

Ineos, a chemical-manufacturing company, was at first faced with a planning refusal for their new headquarters building, which was to replace an undistinguished Victorian house in the Hampshire greenbelt. Fortunately, they persevered and the result is a masterly modern building which, while it makes a more purposeful use of the site, does so in a relaxed and uncrowded manner. Care has been taken with architectural form to minimize the bulk of the building. Single-storey to the east, its zinc-covered concrete roof curves over to a double-height terraced west elevation. Car parking tucked under the large boundary trees leads to a variety of garden courts that build up a strong relationship between the internal and external spaces.

Traditional materials – timber cladding, zinc, render, concrete and glass – are composed in imaginative ways to develop an elegant section which contains a series of generous cellular offices. These are stacked to either open into or overlook a spine of airy and spacious open-plan office. Linked to this spine is a circular timber-clad 'pod'. This contains a staff room on the ground floor and a conference room on the first floor. Changing rooms, showers and a gym offer relaxation, but there is no restaurant as the staff are encouraged to use local facilities.

A shallow plan allows natural ventilation. Complex and well-detailed shading to the west elevation stops summer overheating, while heavy thermal mass and good insulation control internal temperatures. Rooflights between the roof's structural ribs maximize the use of daylight to produce beautifully lit spaces. Well-crafted details, thoughtful environmental design, and an elegant plan and section combine to produce a quality building enjoyed by its occupants and neighbours. It offers a model of how good architecture can create an exciting local working environment in the context of the urban fringe.

CLIENT INEOS
STRUCTURAL ENGINEER PRICE & MYERS
SERVICES ENGINEER ATELIER TEN
LANDSCAPE ARCHITECTS PLINCKE
LANDSCAPE / INDIGO DESIGN
QS JACKSON COLES
CONTRACTOR ERNEST IRELAND
CONSTRUCTION
COST £2.3 MILLION
PHOTOGRAPHER COLIN BURDEN

ROTHERMERE AMERICAN INSTITUTE, UNIVERSITY OF OXFORD .OXFORD .KOHN PEDERSON FOX ASSOCIATES (INTERNATIONAL)

The objective of both the design and client teams was to produce a building that was environmentally sensitive to its historic setting and responsible in its construction process and operation. It is orientated on an east–west axis to maximize control of solar gain. Areas where cooling systems are required, such as the bookstacks, are zoned and individually controlled so they do not impact on or rely upon the performance of the rest of the building, which is predominantly naturally ventilated.

The new building houses a library and reading room for American studies at Oxford University, as well as seminar rooms and studies. The siting of this building is unusual in that it serves the whole university but appears to be part of Mansfield College, which it addresses across a new sunken lawn. Originally a theological college, Mansfield College was designed by Basil Champneys in the late-19th century in the neo-Gothic style: the dialogue between this and the Rothermere American Institute is thought-provoking and each enhances the quality of the other.

The building is good-looking externally, but it is inside that it is truly delightful. The lofty main library space looks south but is shielded from the sun by fixed fretted-glass external louvres; from this space you can look out towards the Portland stone of Mansfield College, but also up towards two floors of elegantly detailed galleries housing workspaces and bookshelves beyond. Top light is beautifully handled and there is a constant play of controlled light and shade. Despite many hard surfaces, acoustics are good. Fair-faced concrete, timber, steel and glass are beautifully detailed, particularly at the level of the reader's carrel. The business of providing a thermally massive, mainly naturally ventilated building appears to be effortlessly handled.

CLIENT OXFORD UNIVERSITY
STRUCTURAL ENGINEER DEWHURST MACFARLANE & PARTNERS
SERVICES ENGINEER BURO HAPPOLD
QS DAVID LANGDON & EVEREST
CONTRACTOR SUNLEY TURRIFF CONSTRUCTION
COST £5.5 MILLION
PHOTOGRAPHER PETER COOK – VIEW

PAINSHILL PARK VISITOR CENTRE
.COBHAM .FEILDEN CLEGG BRADLEY

The Painshill Park Visitor Centre's simple geometric organization reflects the existing walled gardens and clearly responds to the site topography. The main building is locked into a landscaped mound that screens the support buildings from the park beyond, whereas the education building is perched above, creating an intimate tree-house experience for the children using it. The construction of the buildings is confident, intelligently organized, legible and deceptively simple, and clearly demonstrates a responsible approach to environmental issues. Simple details enhance the whole, like the large opening screens connecting the main building to the arcade that will create a summer experience of a building without walls.

The approach to the centre induces a sense of excitement and anticipation from the first glimpse of the finely detailed bridge that forms the gateway to the park. The bridge and simple volumes of the new building, built in untreated oak, are unashamedly 21st century yet remain respectful of the 18th-century setting.

The client is very proud of the building and has immense respect for the architects. Their aspirations have clearly been exceeded. By putting forward a flexible approach at the competition stage, the architects have enabled the client and contractor to contribute to the development of the design and construction of the centre. This has enhanced the quality of the end result and the client's satisfaction with the process of commissioning and building the centre.

CLIENT PAINSHILL PARK TRUST LTD
STRUCTURAL ENGINEER STRUCTURES ONE
SERVICES ENGINEER ATELIER TEN
QS WATERMAN ASSOCIATES
CONTRACTOR GEOFFREY OSBORNE LTD
COST £1.38 MILLION
PHOTOGRAPHER DENNIS GILBERT – VIEW

HOUSE IN ABERDEEN LANE
.LONDON N1 .AZMAN OWENS ARCHITECTS

This is a new-build modernist house made of concrete, timber, limestone and glass. The architects were originally appointed to extend the clients' Victorian house, but when that proved impossible they turned to this site instead. The site is a walled-in space at the end of a run of mews houses on one side and a large house on the other, at the end of an unmade lane. The architects have arranged the house at right-angles to the lane so that its long façade faces west to an enclosed garden and its short side faces the lane in a 'defended' manner with few openings. This means that the house faces inwards on to a newly created courtyard.

A planar assembly of fair-faced concrete walls (inside and out – with an insulated cavity) forms the basis of the composition, which takes the shape of two interlocking cubes. The principal spaces of the house are then sculpted by a second layer of timber elements: cupboards and screens that sometimes touch, sometimes slide past the concrete walls.

The west façade is almost all glass, much of which opens up and all of which, at first-floor level, is covered by hardwood louvre screens. These give a degree of extra privacy and help prevent excessive heat gain. This jewel-like construction has clearly been a labour of love for clients and architects alike.

The differing needs of the six family members have been taken on and dealt with, so that a tidy, pared-down contemporary interior is achieved without the obvious need for obsessive tidiness that often has to accompany this style of living.

SHORTLISTED FOR THE ARCHITECTS' JOURNAL FIRST BUILDING AWARD

CLIENT PRIVATE
STRUCTURAL ENGINEER BRIAN ECKERSLEY
SERVICES ENGINEER MENDICK WARING
CONCRETE CONSULTANT DAVID BENNETT
LANDSCAPE ARCHITECT DEL BOUNO / GAZERWITZ
CONTRACTOR VARBUD CONSTRUCTION CO LTD
COST £540,000
PHOTOGRAPHER KEITH COLLIE

BROADWICK STREET
.LONDON W1 .RICHARD ROGERS PARTNERSHIP

The six-floor building is a prestigious office development in the heart of Soho. The ground and basement levels provide restaurant facilities that will enliven the streetscape when they are completed.

The project sits in the Soho Conservation Area and is bounded by lanes and alleyways on all four sides. The main bulk of the scheme maximizes the site footprint and the large curved roof enclosing two floors of a smaller footprint eases the transition between the more intimate scale of Berwick Street and the larger urban scale of Broadwick Street.

The main entrance to the offices on Broadwick Street leads to a spacious triple-aspect reception spanning the full width of the building. This triple aspect is reiterated on the upper office floors and, pleasingly, the tenant has organized the space planning in a manner that respects this. The fifth-floor three-sided external terrace, which marks the beginning of the set-back from Berwick Street, provides a place for social gathering with views across the Soho skyline. The great arched roof encloses a double-height office level.

The plan and elevation clearly express the distinction between the transparent office space and the solid service cores. The neutral palette of materials – fair-faced concrete, high-performance glass, aluminium and stainless steel – is enlivened by occasional splashes of colour. The energy strategy for the building is well-considered and integrated very discretely.

This building is exemplary in its conception and detailing and especially in demonstrating how an unashamed piece of contemporary architecture can sit comfortably in a conservation area. It shows, unlike many of its neighbours, that new architecture doesn't have to be pastiche. This building will have a much longer life and appeal than most of the other 'new' buildings in the area.

CLIENT DERWENT VALLEY
STRUCTURAL ENGINEER ARUP
SERVICES ENGINEER BDSP
QS DAVIS LANGDON & EVEREST
CONTRACTOR JOHN SISK & SON
COST £6.9 MILLION
PHOTOGRAPHERS PETER CAMPBELL (LEFT); RICHARD BRYANT – ARCAID (RIGHT)

THE CHARTER SCHOOL
.LONDON SE24 .PENOYRE & PRASAD

This is a complicated refurbishment with inserted rebuilding of one of Leslie Martin's London County Council secondary schools. There are areas where the original design is respected and areas where it is rejected as obsolete. The architects have responded well to a complex brief and the new design, as well as the subtly staged programme for its delivery, fit both the needs of the school, staff and students and planned future growth. The new entrance hall and foyer are key to the organization of the spaces and aid orientation. The result is a useable space with a pleasant acoustic. The commitment to sustainability is demonstrated by the use of rainwater recycled as grey water to flush the WCs.

The judges were particularly impressed by the school's exemplary approach to security and accessibility. Here the design meets the stated needs with imagination, so that students are made to feel that the security-card system is a process enabling inclusion rather than causing exclusion.

The building manager has clearly bought into this innovative programme, responding with a positive attitude that he shares with the staff, students and visitors to the school. The students themselves are more than willing to talk about how much they enjoy their school and how involved with it they feel.

The school sits on the original site but the new entrance is well placed and the associated landscaping works effectively in providing a spatial context.

CLIENT SOUTHWARK COUNCIL
STRUCTURAL ENGINEER BABTIE
SERVICES ENGINEER SOUTHWARK BUILDING DESIGN SERVICE
LANDSCAPE ARCHITECT WATKINS DALLY
QS FRANKLIN & ANDREWS
CONTRACTOR MANSELL CONSTRUCTION SERVICES LTD
COST £17 MILLION
PHOTOGRAPHER KILLIAN O'SULLIVAN

CHISWICK PARK
.LONDON W4 .RICHARD ROGERS PARTNERSHIP

The first phases of this major new business and urban park comprise six four-storey buildings with undercrofts (containing car parking and plant rooms). The buildings provide accommodation in the form of offices, health club, swimming pool, and brasserie/café, all set in a generous landscaped public space that includes an open-air performance area and a lake. Vehicles have been excluded from the centre of the development, ensuring a pleasant environment for the users of the buildings as well as open access for the public.

Environmentally, the combined system of fixed high-level anodized-aluminium louvres and retractable external fabric blinds, automatically activated by light sensors, shades 90 per cent of the buildings' surfaces and works very well. The landscape also assists environmental controls, with the lake collecting rainwater run-off from the roofs.

The simplicity of the buildings is concealed by the textural nature of the external screening and walkways. These add visual interest as well as having a practical purpose, significantly reducing the requirement for air-cooling. The clarity of the building plan – a central core surrounded by office plates – was assisted by the use of external escape stairs, allowing clear open spaces to the perimeter of 18 metres from the core. The usually forgotten spaces such as toilets and, in particular, the undercroft areas, are as considered and as well-delivered as the more public areas.

The quality of the materials and the attention to detail throughout is pleasingly apparent. The client clearly takes pride in the project and the quality of maintenance of the landscape is exemplary. This project is an excellent example to developers throughout the UK, clearly demonstrating that a simple, well-conceived project on this scale can be achieved within a reasonable cost.

CLIENT STANHOPE PLC
STRUCTURAL ENGINEER ARUP
LANDSCAPE ARCHITECT WEST 8
QS DAVIS LANGDON & EVEREST
CONTRACTOR BOVIS CONSTRUCTION
COST £130 MILLION
PHOTOGRAPHER GRANT SMITH

CLEARWATER YARD
.LONDON NW1 .ALLFORD HALL MONAGHAN MORRIS

The site for this ingenious speculative office development is a former timberyard, incongruously located in the middle of Georgian terraced houses and a primary school. Existing planning permission helped determine the general footprint and height restrictions. A very irregularly shaped site, a multitude of concerned neighbours and the financial imperative to maximize lettable floor area have lead to an unusual solution, one that provides a calm oasis in the city.

This is architect and enlightened client in harmony, finding a clear solution to a difficult problem. All that shows from the street is a large metal slab with a horizontal viewing slot at eye level providing a sneak preview of the delightful inner space. In effect, this is a narrow, descending courtyard leading to an entrance about 2 metres lower than general ground level, enabling three floors of offices to be inserted without exceeding the planning height restrictions.

The building is only able to have windows facing into the courtyard. These façades are made up of a combination of full-height balustrade-strength windows, panels of translucent glass channels (Reglit) and green full-height metal panels that open for ventilation. The result is a bright, comfortable and peaceful working environment.

The roofs of the development are nearly flat and are planted with sedums, grasses, flowers and mosses. This green solution is not only environmentally sound, it is also, just as importantly, much appreciated by all the neighbours.

CLIENT LATITUDE INVESTMENTS LTD
STRUCTURAL ENGINEER TECHNIKER
SERVICES ENGINEER MONSAL ASSOCIATES
QS THOMSON CLIFFORD PARTNERSHIP
CONTRACTOR DURKAN PUDELEK
COST £2 MILLION
PHOTOGRAPHER TIMOTHY SOAR

HAMPSTEAD THEATRE
.LONDON NW3 .BENNETTS ASSOCIATES

Hampstead Theatre is the first freestanding theatre to be built in London since Lasdun's National in 1975, and the first to be built specifically for the production of contemporary drama. It has been designed to support the theatre's tradition of fostering new writing, with a flexible stage and a compact auditorium that can adapt to each play and production.

The diagram of the building is clear and simple. It has a 'Tardis' quality: the architect has cleverly managed to insert a 325-seat auditorium, rehearsal facilities, flexible education space, bar, box office, office, technical and storage areas, and dressing rooms into a relatively small footprint, without making the spaces feel cramped. Remarkably, the building has an intimacy in keeping with the historic tradition of the original Hampstead Theatre.

The external horizontal timber screens create visual texture, especially at night, and the reappearance of this horizontal detail inside the auditorium reinforces the integrity of the building as a whole. The thrusting prow of the auditorium and the way it pierces the roof create a dramatic statement.

The internal public spaces encourage exploration and there are many opportunities for patrons to see and be seen. The auditorium has a delightful intimacy and warmth. The integration of complicated technical staging systems has been accommodated without impinging on the appearance of the space. The flexibility – not least in the provision of wheelchair spaces – designed into the auditorium will serve the theatre well.

This is a building that will mature with dignity and as the external masterplan is completed it will become a major hub for the local community. Disabled access has been carefully considered and in a very inclusive manner. The client deserves credit for its role in creating such an environment and fostering an excellent piece of architecture.

SHORTLISTED FOR THE ADAPT TRUST ACCESS AWARD

CLIENT HAMPSTEAD THEATRE
STRUCTURAL ENGINEER CURTINS CONSULTING
SERVICES ENGINEER ERNEST GRIFFITHS & SON
THEATRE CONSULTANT THEATREPLAN
ACOUSTICS CONSULTANT ARUP ACOUSTICS
LIGHTING ARTWORKS MARTIN RICHMAN
QS CITEX BUCKNALL AUSTIN
CONTRACTOR DOVE BROTHERS LTD
COST £8 MILLION
PHOTOGRAPHER PETER COOK – VIEW

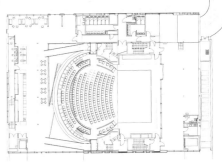

GROUND-FLOOR PLAN

JUBILEE SCHOOL
.LONDON SW2 .ALLFORD HALL MONAGHAN MORRIS

This was a complex project involving the closure of three existing schools – two primary schools and one for profoundly deaf children – and co-locating them on one of the sites. From the outset, the aim was to re-examine and redefine conventional usage and the perceptions of schools and their facilities. The consultation process was almost as important as the design process, as the closure of any school is a sensitive matter.

The school is located on a main road with housing on three sides, providing a new and colourful local landmark. Sustainability as an approach has been fundamental to the building's design. The architects have adopted a low-energy approach both to the building's fabric and its maintenance. All classrooms are naturally ventilated, using a chimney that also admits light. But the most visually striking thing about the school is the colourful result of a series of collaborations with artists, graphic designers and furniture designers. Light artist Martin Richman has used light and colour to help define routes and usage throughout the building; Studio Myerscough has developed a strong and boldly applied corporate identity for the school; and Andrew Stafford has designed a furniture range which includes a prototype chair whose size is determined by the age group.

There is an eagerness about the children here that is not always evident in schools. On the first day of term teachers were forced to do a head count to ensure siblings had not stayed behind rather than going off to their own schools: a number of fraudsters were discovered.

The design vision for the school and the 'new deal' for schools generally is manifest in this project. It is reflected in all aspects of the design, including the detailing, the openness and cheerfulness of the whole place. All of this has been achieved within a tight budget.

CLIENT LONDON BOROUGH OF LAMBETH EDUCATION DEPARTMENT
ARTIST MARTIN RICHMAN
GRAPHIC DESIGNER STUDIO MYERSCOUGH
FURNITURE DESIGNER ANDREW STAFFORD
STRUCTURAL ENGINEER ELLIOT WOOD PARTNERSHIP
SERVICES ENGINEER ATELIER TEN
QS THE COOK & BUTLER PARTNERSHIP
CONTRACTOR BALLAST CONSTRUCTION
COST £5 MILLION
PHOTOGRAPHER TIMOTHY SOAR

MILLENNIUM BRIDGE
.LINKING THE CITY OF LONDON WITH SOUTHWARK
.FOSTER & PARTNERS

The Millennium Bridge was the result of a design competition for a pedestrian bridge across the Thames. It is the world's longest pedestrian suspension bridge and the first completely new bridge of any kind over the Thames for more than a hundred years. 350 metres long, it links the City and St Paul's Cathedral on the north bank of the Thames with Tate Modern on the south bank.

Free of traffic and accessible to everyone 24 hours a day, it is estimated that 4 million people will use the bridge every year. As well as being a means of getting from A to B (and what an A and what a B), the bridge is a destination in its own right, affording Londoners a place to promenade and enjoy unrivalled views of the capital. It is one of those rare things – like the London Eye – a piece of architecture that changes not only the way people see their city but also the way they use it.

Now famous, this suspension bridge pushes materials to the limit in order to produce the most slender, elegant object imaginable. Instead of holding its arms in the air to support its suspension cables, it has them at full stretch horizontally – try it and see what hard work that is. The result when viewed from downstream is so thin as to be hardly there. Close up, it is a wonderful assembly of almost organic components that provide an ever-changing composition, reminding one of a 21st-century version of something that might be seen in the Natural History Museum.

Credit for the structure must go not only to Chris Wise, who led the original Arup team, but also to Tony Fitzpatrick, who led the remedial work. Sadly this was one of Tony's last major projects; he was killed while riding his bicycle in the US in the summer of 2003.

CLIENT LONDON BOROUGH OF SOUTHWARK
SCULPTOR SIR ANTHONY CARO
STRUCTURAL ENGINEER ARUP
SERVICES ENGINEER ARUP
LIGHTING ENGINEERS CLAUDE ENGLE / ARUP
QS DAVIS LANGDON & EVEREST
CONTRACTORS MONBERG & THORSEN MCALPINE JOINT VENTURE (MAIN BRIDGE WORKS) / BALFOUR BEATTY CONSTRUCTION LTD (PRELIMINARY WORKS)
COST £14 MILLION
PHOTOGRAPHER NIGEL YOUNG

SECTION

163 .LONDON

QUEEN'S GALLERY, BUCKINGHAM PALACE .LONDON SW1 .JOHN SIMPSON & PARTNERS

A growing desire to make more of the royal collection easily accessible to the public and to provide a better setting for temporary exhibitions, coupled with the need to improve the royal kitchens, lay behind the creation of the new Queen's Gallery at Buckingham Palace.

The original gallery, opened in the 1960s, was an unsatisfactory space with inadequate climate controls. Located in the former chapel, it was linked by a long corridor to an anonymous entrance on Buckingham Palace Road. The new scheme provides three large galleries, three smaller exhibition spaces, an education room and a lecture hall, together with an entrance hall, shop and a distinctive street frontage. This is partly achieved by making use of existing space, partly by extending unobtrusively into the garden. Underneath the lecture hall is the remodelled palace kitchen, part of a major reorganisation of the palace's service arrangements. John Simpson has devoted as much care and attention to these parts of the scheme, which are unseen by the public, as to the more visible parts.

Simpson's scheme is robustly classical, developing the rich language of the late Greek revival to create a deliberately palatial setting for the exhibits. The bold entrance portico, the entrance hall and the elevation of the pavilion overlooking the gardens of Buckingham Palace take forward Simpson's interest in early Greek architecture, particularly that of Paestum. The galleries draw more directly on John Nash's original Buckingham Palace interiors. Classical detailing is also skilfully used to overcome difficulties with a complex site and to integrate mechanical services unobtrusively into the building. The scheme includes an extensive decorative programme in the entrance hall by the classical sculptor, Alexander Stoddart.

CLIENT DIRECTOR OF PROPERTY SERVICES, BUCKINGHAM PALACE
STRUCTURAL ENGINEER GIFFORD & PARTNERS
SERVICES ENGINEER FABER MAUNSELL
QS HUNTLEY CARTWRIGHT
CONTRACTOR WATES CONSTRUCTION
COST £20.6 MILLION
PHOTOGRAPHER THE ROYAL COLLECTION

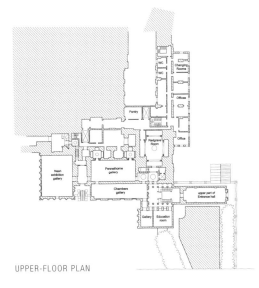

UPPER-FLOOR PLAN

RAWSTHORNE PLACE
.LONDON EC1 .BENNETTS ASSOCIATES WITH BAYNES & MITCHELL

The project involved the reuse of an irregularly shaped piece of land and buildings surrounded by Georgian and early-Victorian houses. The run-down collection of buildings on the site included a former printworks and an 18th-century barn – a unique survivor from the days when livestock required a resting place on their way to Smithfield Market.

In line with this practice's general approach to sustainable construction, they have nurtured the old buildings back into life and skilfully knitted the whole together with contemporary and sympathetic new elements, creating a place that is naturally ventilated, with low-embedded-energy, and delightful to work in. The journey around the project is full of changes – clean efficient electronic office one moment, then the next it's the ancient brickwork and timber of the cowshed, followed by the concrete and steel of the printworks. The roofs of the new elements are thermally efficient 'green' surfaces planted with sedum. This, along with the carefully handled negotiation process with the building's many neighbours, has made it a welcome addition to the area. The project is the subject of an in-depth post-occupancy evaluation carried out by the Building Research Establishment.

Rawsthorne Place is a good example of the kind of practical conservation for which our cities are crying out: the careful piecing back together of run-down neighbourhoods using a mix of restoration and counterpointing new-build. Here there may have been no client to satisfy – the scheme houses the architect's own offices – but there will be plenty of future ones who may be inspired to commission similar work during visits to the practice.

CLIENT RAB BENNETTS
CONSERVATION ADVISER RICHARD GRIFFITHS
STRUCTURAL ENGINEER PRICE & MYERS
SERVICES ENGINEER CUNDALL JOHNSON & PARTNERS
QS MICHAEL LATHAM ASSOCIATES
CONTRACTOR SAMES
COST £1.2 MILLION
PHOTOGRAPHER BENNETTS ASSOCIATES

THE RED HOUSE
.LONDON SW3 .TONY FRETTON ARCHITECTS

The house was commissioned as a place to live in and in which to display the client's collection of contemporary art; it was always intended as a work of art in its own right, to rank alongside significant European houses past and present. Pre-existing planning permission allowed for the replacement of two 1850s cottages by one large house. The new house is on five storeys, with a floor area of 655 square metres. A ground-floor garage with sliding stone doors is flanked by a main entrance and the entrance to the staff apartment. The principal rooms – a classically scaled living room and a more intimate sitting room – are on the first floor and are double-height. Above is a mezzanine library, with the bedrooms and their bathrooms arranged round a roof garden and hothouse on the top floor. The structure is reinforced concrete with a rainscreen of eponymous red limestone from France.

The plan is highly innovative, particularly in the relationship between the grand rooms and the intimate ones. Amid the grandeur and formality, the sudden intimacy of spaces such as the office/library is a surprise. The result is that space is used in a full and meaningful way.

Tite Street is in a conservation area, with houses of very varied styles. As such, the new house sits well, adding yet another style to the streetscape. The generosity of frontage also benefits the street. To the rear, the house backs on to the gardens of Wren's Royal Hospital, and the salon's great windows enjoy this to the full.

This a generous, even indulgent house, built for a contemporary benefactor and art patron. It is also a deeply personal one and this is reflected in all aspects of the design, including the presentation of the art and the design of the furniture.

SHORTLISTED FOR THE MANSER MEDAL

CLIENT PRIVATE
INTERIOR DESIGNER STUDIO MARK PIMLOTT
STRUCTURAL ENGINEER PRICE & MYERS
SERVICES ENGINEER FULCRUM ENGINEERING
LANDSCAPE ARCHITECT JULIE TOLL LANDSCAPE
STONE CONSULTANT HARRISON GOLDMAN
QS DAVIS LANGDON & EVEREST
CONTRACTOR BLUESTONE PLC
COST £3.5 MILLION
PHOTOGRAPHER HÉLÈNE BINET

THE WOMEN'S LIBRARY
.LONDON E1 .WRIGHT & WRIGHT ARCHITECTS

This building, in the heart of the East End, was developed to house the internationally significant Fawcett Library Collection. The scheme comprises an exhibition hall, seminar room, educational facilities, reading room, archives, café, offices, friends' room, and garden.

The starting point is a retained façade of the Victorian wash-house that stood on the site – a fitting memory to women's work in the 19th century and the struggles to come in the 20th century. The volumes of the new project are subtly layered back from this historical introduction – clearly expressing the juxtaposition of old and new, while also expressing the spatial system of the building. The new building, in keeping with its Victorian progenitor, is heavy and robust, with a carefully controlled palette of materials: beautifully laid hand-made red brick with light-coloured lime/sand mortar, oak, stone, steel and glass. As well as being expressive of and appropriate to the former use of the site, the heavy construction suits the low-energy natural environmental controls built into the scheme. Even the archives, which contain valuable documents, are passively controlled both in respect of temperature and humidity – it is estimated to consume no more than 20 per cent of the energy of a conventional system. Although the archives' environment has to be passively controlled, the use of heavy concrete blocks reduces temperature and humidity fluctuations. Where possible, the spaces are naturally ventilated with opening windows. Daylight is supplemented with movement-sensitive low-energy lighting systems.

This lovingly crafted work has been carefully constructed and is much-appreciated by its users. Some entirely appropriate architectural references are openly stated – summing up the overall integrity of the project.

CLIENT THE WOMEN'S LIBRARY
STRUCTURAL ENGINEER ARUP
SERVICES ENGINEER ARUP
QS DAVIS LANGDON & EVEREST
CONTRACTOR KIER LONDON
COST £4.7 MILLION
PHOTOGRAPHER PETER COOK – VIEW

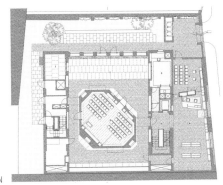

GROUND-FLOOR PLAN

YOUNG HOUSE
.LONDON W11 .TONKIN LIU

A typical mews house in central London has been transformed by the architect into a unique environment where light is the key. By day the exterior appears unremarkable in the mews. At night the interior takes on an almost kaleidoscopic appearance, creating a powerful impression from the outside and a memorable experience from within. At the client's first briefing the architect was shown an image of a James Turrell light-art installation as the inspiration. The client wanted a 'house made of light' and, delightfully, the result lives up to this first aspiration.

The initial jury felt that a daytime visit was essential to prove that this was no mere 'lighting job'. On arrival they were quickly reassured: the almost totally white interior and the cutting back of the two floor slabs ensure that the interior is suffused with natural light, making it a beautiful space.

The architect has described the project as a house with three towers: the lower tower for sleeping, the tallest tower for moving around in and the middle tower for cooking and washing. This was less apparent in reality than it was on paper. The use of a gloss resin on each of the floors provides a further reflective surface upon which light can play and be reflected. The client has got good value for his investment – only £120,000 – and this fact deserves to be broadcast. All of this has been achieved by careful design and simple detailing that has produced an uplifting experience.

SHORTLISTED FOR THE STEPHEN LAWRENCE PRIZE

CLIENT PRIVATE
STRUCTURAL ENGINEER MIKE HADI ASSOCIATES
LIGHTING CONSULTANT DAN HEAP, MIND'S EYE
CONTRACTOR CAPITAL REFURBISHMENT LTD
COST £120,000
PHOTOGRAPHER JEFFERSON SMITH – ARCBLUE

BIOLOGICAL RESEARCH LABORATORIES
.BIBERACH, GERMANY .SAUERBRUCH HUTTON

This building contains laboratories, offices and meeting rooms for pharmaceutical research on a secure campus. The brief was to provide high-quality facilities for staff and to make a building whose presence could be used to promote the forward-looking aspirations of the company. A central corridor gives access to perimeter rooms on six floors. The depth of the building allows natural ventilation from both sides, although the laboratories use dedicated mechanical ventilation to support specialist processes. All services rise through a single concrete core that forms a sheer wall along one side of the central corridor.

The edge of the building is given up to special treatment and this is where much of the architect's trademark inventiveness has been applied. There is a two-layer external wall. The inner layer is of solid insulated construction with strip windows bringing air and light to the workspaces. The external layer is made from glass panels that have a dense matrix of coloured dots printed on the surface. The panels open and shut automatically to control direct sunlight and moderate heat and glare. From the outside the building appears as a sheer block composed of different coloured panels. Seen from within, the panels are translucent and they give to each workspace a different quality of light depending on the colour of the dots. If you open a window in the inner layer and look out into the space between the two skins you get a marvellous view of the spectrum of colours on all the panels and of the weird array of pistons that operate the system.

This idea is really very simple but it doesn't appear slight. It looks surprisingly lovely from the inside. From the outside, where a clearly graphic impact is intended, it is a cool multi-coloured array. It has been carried off with great conviction. The judges were told that it was meant to refer to coloured spectrographs. Perhaps it looks like candy-coloured stacks of pharmaceutical boxes. It does occupy a strange territory between robust function and gay frivolity. Serious science, like strong medicine, is made to look like kids' sweets.

CLIENT BOEHRINGER INGELHEIM PHARMA KG
STRUCTURAL ENGINEER KREBS UND KIEFER
SERVICES ENGINEER ZIBELL WILLNER & PARTNER
GLASS FAÇADE M&V
CONTRACTOR GEORG REISCH GMBH & CO KG
COST £11.9 MILLION
PHOTOGRAPHERS GERRIT ENGEL FOTOGRAFIE; JAN BITTER (BOTTOM RIGHT)

175 .EUROPEAN UNION

CENTRE FOR RESEARCH INTO INFECTIOUS DISEASES .UNIVERSITY COLLEGE DUBLIN .DUBLIN, IRELAND .O'DONNELL + TUOMEY

The research laboratories are housed in a landmark building overlooking Dublin Bay. The site is a sloping and sheltered part of the wooded Belfield campus of University College Dublin, a campus until recently more noted for its natural beauty than its architecture.

The brief was for a building with two distinct functions: a research institute for highly specialized investigations into medical microbiology, and laboratories for the routine testing of medical samples. As a result (and somewhat confusingly) there are two entrances. The one best signed and most used is the least impressive and leads off the car park into the single-storey laboratories that completely enclose a landscaped internal courtyard. The scale is determined by a nondescript building that might have been replaced given a more generous budget.

The main laboratory block is far more representative of O'Donnell and Tuomey's work, demonstrating their customary imagination and skill in composition and providing a significant landmark in its own right, clearly visible upon entering the campus. The entrance here is almost grandiloquent but may prove fully justified when the circulation in this part of the campus is finalized. The block is carried on slim steel columns, making its massing all the more dramatic; the uniform dark cladding of the façades adds to the impact of the form.

Internally, the arrangement of laboratories in the north-facing tower element is particularly successful in delivering generous spaces, with full-height glazing giving good views over the mature landscape of the campus.

Overall, the building represents an exciting and innovative solution to the technical and spatial programme, while providing an enjoyable workplace.

CLIENT UNIVERSITY COLLEGE DUBLIN
STRUCTURAL ENGINEER ARUP
SERVICES ENGINEER ARUP
QS BOYD & CREED
CONTRACTOR TOWNLINK CONSTRUCTION LTD
COST € 4 MILLION
PHOTOGRAPHER DENNIS GILBERT – VIEW

HISTORY MUSEUM AND MUSIC SCHOOL EXTENSION .STUTTGART, GERMANY .WILFORD SCHUPP ARCHITEKTEN / MICHAEL WILFORD & PARTNERS

The scheme includes the History Museum and an extension to the Music School that won the Stirling Prize in 1997, and it completes the composition of cultural buildings started by Stirling and Wilford's seminal Staatsgalerie in 1984. The original building set up a north–south promenade between the densely trafficked Konrad-Adenauer-Strasse and the rotunda-centred body of the gallery. A side road, Eugenstrasse, which used to lead on to the main road and cut the site in two, has, with the completion of the new building, been turned into a public square, framed by the earlier building to the north and the new museum to the south.

The museum is on six floors and provides permanent and travelling exhibition space, with all the supporting facilities. A generous foyer houses information desk and shop and leads to the café and, via a grand staircase, to the exhibition spaces – the spine of the new building. The route culminates in a top-floor gallery that opens out on to a roof terrace with superb views of the city. This is used as an outside exhibition area.

A further public square has been created south of the new museum, this time framed by the new building and the Music School. To a large measure, the success of this project is in the creation of external spaces relating to the city of Stuttgart beyond and binding the three phases of the development together.

Externally, the architecture of the new building echoes but subtly updates the design of its predecessors, being of stone and stucco, counterpointed by pink and purple metalwork. The arrival sequence is elegantly handled and uses display/sculptural elements to great effect to blur the distinction between inside and out. The interior of the building plan is essentially simple and legible, with the permanent display separated from the temporary display by a fine top-lit straight-flight stair. A mature piece of architecture.

CLIENT LAND BADEN-WÜRTTEMBERG
STRUCTURAL ENGINEER BOLL + PARTNER
SERVICES ENGINEER JAEGER, MORNHINWEG & PARTNER
CONTRACTOR LEONHARD WEISS GMBH
COST €33.5 MILLION
PHOTOGRAPHERS ALBRECHT SCHNABEL (LEFT); MARTIN BRAUN (RIGHT)

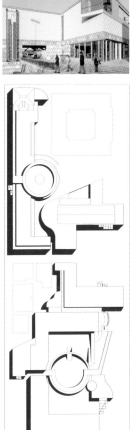

SITE PLAN

OFFALY COUNTY COUNCIL CIVIC OFFICES
.TULLAMORE, IRELAND .ABK ARCHITECTS

This headquarters for Offaly County Council, on one of the main approaches to the town of Tullamore in the Irish midlands, represents a new public face for a forward-looking council. It also represents a very good case study in effective briefing, an open creative dialogue between client and architect during the design process leading to the successful procurement of a fine building. Over a period of 18 months, 5200 square metres of accommodation have been constructed at a cost of £10.5 million. The building contains general office space and a laboratory, a council chamber for the elected representatives, a café and a crèche for staff and the local community arranged around an atrium that accommodates exhibitions and general community functions.

A monumental hardwood lattice forms a veil around the primary office space, affording protection from the over-heating effects of the sun, and externally blurring the boundary between the building and the landscape of mature woodland. The council chamber, by contrast, is expressed in monumental panels of Carlow limestone. This urban/rural dichotomy matches the character of the town itself. The council chamber, with its literal echoes of Finnish precedent, draws timber inside the building.

The council has moved from buildings that represented closed local government to buildings that are welcoming and generous. This is most evident in the triple-height top-lit atrium on to which the various departments have their own reception points. The building on either side of this perspectival street is a three-storey in-situ concrete-framed volume clad externally in timber and glass that was conceived as a pavilion in its landscape setting. The offices are an example of well-detailed and ordered design, where, for example, the in-situ concrete soffits and structural columns accommodate services seamlessly. The floor slabs incorporate coils that use groundwater from subterranean sources for cooling the building in summer and heating it in winter.

SHORTLISTED FOR THE RIBA JOURNAL SUSTAINABILITY AWARD

CLIENT OFFALY COUNTY COUNCIL
STRUCTURAL ENGINEER MICHAEL PUNCH & PARTNERS
SERVICES ENGINEER HOMAN O'BRIEN
QS DAVIS LANGDON PKS
CONTRACTOR JOHN SISK & SONS
COST €16 MILLION
PHOTOGRAPHER CHRISTIAN RICHTERS

PRIVATE HOUSE IN GALICIA
.CORRUBEDO, SPAIN .DAVID CHIPPERFIELD ARCHITECTS WITH CARLOS SEOANE

A robust, relatively cheap holiday home large enough for two families, but at the same time a significant work of modern architecture, David Chipperfield's house fits easily into its picturesque context while not compromising its architectural vision. The house is built on the edge of the workaday Galician fishing village of Corrubedo, in a gap in a street of houses, sitting directly above the sea with a dramatic view over a wide bay to the south. Unlike traditional houses in the village, it does not turn its back on the sea but makes the most of the views with large windows and balconies. By contrast, the street elevation is unassertive, almost anonymous, as if not wanting to draw attention to itself.

The street front lies in the angle of a bend in the road and takes its line and massing from the adjacent houses, one two-storey, the other three-storey, and each set at very different angles. This divides the house into two distinct elements at the upper level, with a bedroom and roof terrace above on one side, and bedroom and study above on the other. The bedrooms are linked by a large balcony in the angle whose rectangular projecting form is the dominant element on the south elevation. Below the bedrooms, approached up a half flight of stairs from the street and taking up the width of the house, is the living room and kitchen. This has a completely glazed elevation facing the bay. A shower room and three children's rooms, tightly but efficiently designed with bunk beds, with storage in the corridor behind, are set in the stone plinth of the building, with direct access to the beach.

The palette of materials and colours in the house is restrained: white rendered internal and external walls, terracotta floors, marble sills to the windows and simple wooden furniture designed by the architect. The feel of the building is that of a well-used holiday home, not a self-conscious architectural insertion into a traditional village.

SHORTLISTED FOR THE STEPHEN LAWRENCE PRIZE

CLIENT PRIVATE
STRUCTURAL ENGINEER JAVIER ESTEVEZ CIMADEVILLA
CONTRACTOR SERINFRA SA
COST £200,000
PHOTOGRAPHER HÉLÈNE BINET

GROUND-FLOOR PLAN

Living Room & Kitchen

Entrance

183 .EUROPEAN UNION

ST JOSEPH'S HOSPITAL
.CORK, IRELAND .BUILDING DESIGN PARTNERSHIP

BDP was asked to provide a secure yet stimulating environment for the various residents of this private hospital for the elderly on the outskirts of Cork. Seven flats for long-term patients and 62 high-dependency bedrooms with en-suite bathrooms are provided in a series of fingers radiating from a curved main street. Each terminates in a cedar-clad lounge. The design enhances both a sense of community and of distinctiveness. Externally, the clusters of buildings cling to the hillside like the houses of a Greek village. The choice of materials reflects the local vernacular: white rendered walls and peat-brown clay tiles give an authentic village feel to the place, with zinc used to highlight the rooflines. Cedar is used inside and out, and appropriately so, as it is known to be an analgesic and can contribute to the healing process.

The buildings have been arranged on the site with care and sensitivity to meet the needs of the residents and staff who use the centre. The architects have challenged traditional concepts of circulation space and created an internal environment that encourages informality and interaction. Circulation areas are generous, naturally lit and arranged to create sitting and meeting areas. Residential accommodation is similarly carefully planned to form spaces that allow the maximum enjoyment of views and light for residents, many of whom spend their days in bed or sitting in armchairs. The social focuses of the project are the dining room and chapel, both of which are well-proportioned and enjoyable meeting spaces.

The project's greatest success is the creation of an environment that provides quality of life and dignity to people with a range of physical and mental disabilities.

CLIENT BON SECOURS HEALTH SYSTEM
ENGINEER JOHN O'DONOVAN & ASSOCIATES
LANDSCAPE ARCHITECT BUILDING DESIGN PARTNERSHIP
QS BRUCE SHAW PARTNERSHIP
CONTRACTOR ROHCON LTD
COST €11.77 MILLION
PHOTOGRAPHER KEITH HUNTER

SOCIAL HOUSING
.GALBALLY, IRELAND .O'DONNELL + TUOMEY

This project provides two terraces of new social housing in the village of
Galbally, a 19th-century planned village with a consistent urban character.
Each building steps from the next, but the overall building line slopes with the
contour of the site. The entrance to each house has been designed to provide
a seat, planting box and threshold, all cast in terrazzo within a recessed
porch, providing a semi-private, semi-public mediation between house and
village. Each dwelling has a large cutaway balcony – double-height in the
case of the houses – painted in a range of fired-earth colours. Far from being
gratuitous, this use of colour is a subtle take on the garish paints used these
days to identify the individual terraced houses in so many Celtic villages from
West Cork to Cornwall or the Isle of Mull.

The success of the project lies in the simplicity and sophistication with which
traditional domestic form and details are reinterpreted. One terrace provides
six three-storey houses that cleverly take advantage of the sloping site to
create an unusual and interesting house type. The lower level and first floor
both have access to external areas. While the generous balconies mean
losing internal floor area, they do create a strong, articulated and colourful
frontage to the terrace.

The smaller terrace provides five single-storey dwellings, again reinterpreting
traditional terraces under a single sloping roof. This block succeeds in
continuing the streetscape of Galbally and reinforcing the urban grain.
The detailing of the project is impressive; in particular, the robust handling
of windows, balconies and chimneys creates an impression of durability
and quality.

The project is not only a success architecturally but also seems to be enjoyed
and valued by the people who live in it.

CLIENT LIMERICK COUNTY COUNCIL
STRUCTURAL ENGINEER MICHAEL PUNCH &
PARTNERS
CONTRACTOR KYLE CIVIL ENGINEERING
LTD
COST €2.3 MILLION
PHOTOGRAPHER ROS KAVANAGH

PLANS: SINGLE-STOREY
HOUSE (RIGHT) AND THREE-
STOREY HOUSE (BELOW)

187 .EUROPEAN UNION

WORLD TRADE CENTRE .AMSTERDAM, THE NETHERLANDS .KOHN PEDERSON FOX ASSOCIATES (INTERNATIONAL)

The brief to the architect was to up-date a group of glazed office buildings designed and completed in the early 1980s. Typical for their period, the buildings were relatively hermetic, and the complex bore little relationship to any immediate or wider urban grain. Following a preliminary study into relatively modest improvements, a wider investment was agreed that would add public and social dimensions, reclad the existing buildings without major interruptions to tenants, and provide an additional 45,000 square metres of office space, doubling the centre's capacity.

The project, undertaken in conjunction with the city landscape authorities, creates a new public square (yet to be completed), and pedestrian links through the buildings. Internally, the vast atrium is a cross between a corporate reception and a public street. It houses, as well as reception facilities, high-street shops and restaurants that really do draw shoppers into what would otherwise be a closed world. This incorporation of public uses into private space creates a lively atmosphere much removed from what could otherwise have been a dull, monocultural space.

The roof, engineered in consultation with Battle McCarthy, is essentially a freestanding structure, wrapping round the office buildings but structurally independent of them. It is formed of structural blades spanning up to 21 metres, functioning as weather protection and providing solar and acoustic control, lighting and fire protection. The new tower is fitted with internal timber screens for independent solar control. These produce a strongly textured appearance.

A variety of working environments has been provided, but a sense of order pervades the project as a whole. The linking of some office floors has helped to create an intimate atmosphere for tenants, rather than layered separation. Environmentally friendly systems have been introduced in a welcome manner. Overall, the attempt to create a sense of place, to provide coherence across the complex as a whole, and to relate it to the urban grain beyond its context is a great success.

CLIENTS ING VASTGOED / KANTOREN FONDS NEDERLAND MANAGEMENT BV / WTC AMSTERDAM REAL ESTATE
STRUCTURAL ENGINEERS VAN ROSSUM RAADGEVENDE INGENIEURS AMSTERDAM / RFR PARIS
SERVICES ENGINEERS BATTLE MCCARTHY / TECHNICAL MANAGEMENT
QS BASALT BOUWADVIES
CONTRACTOR BOUWCOMBINATIE ZUIDPLEIN
COST £44 MILLION
PHOTOGRAPHER H G ESCH

LISTS AND SPONSORS

ASSESSORS

The RIBA is extremely grateful to the assessors, all of whom, both architects and non-architects, give their time freely and whose reports form the basis of much of the text of this book.

THE STIRLING PRIZE JURY 2003
George Ferguson – RIBA President (chair)
Isabel Allen – Editor of *The Architects' Journal*
Julian Barnes – novelist
Justine Frischmann – singer and TV presenter
Chris Wilkinson – architect, Stirling winner 2001 and 2002

THE RIBA AWARDS GROUP JUDGES 2003
Eric Parry (chair)
Tony Chapman
Roger Bright
Paul Finch
Kathryn Findlay
Glenn Howells
Louisa Hutton
Niall McLaughlin
David Page
Jeremy Till
Joanna van Heyningen
Giles Worsley

REGIONAL ASSESSORS – RIBA AWARDS 2003
The judges are listed in the following order:
chair of jury (nationally appointed architect)
lay juror
regional representative (architect from region)

SCOTLAND
Edward Cullinan, Martin Spring, Jack Fulton

NORTHERN IRELAND
Niall Phillips, Richard Bryant, Clyde Markwell

NORTH
Richard Parnaby, Michael Rose, Peter Beacock

NORTH WEST
Richard Murphy, Mark Whitby, Ian Banks

YORKSHIRE
Richard Parnaby, Michael Rose, John Edmonds

WALES
Ian Standing, Beatrix Campbell, Chris Loyn
(no awards made in 2003)

WEST MIDLANDS
Malcolm Fraser, Stephen Feber, Alan McBeth

EAST MIDLANDS
Malcolm Fraser, Stephen Feber, Rima Yousif
(no awards made in 2003)

EAST
Kathryn Findlay, Louise Todd, Peter Goodwin

SOUTH WEST
Anthony McGuirk, Frances Sorrell, Jonathan Ball

WESSEX
Anthony McGuirk, Frances Sorrell, Nigel Begg

SOUTH
Malcolm Parry, Kim Wilkie, Colin James

SOUTH EAST
Graham Stirk, John Sorrell, Mike Lawless

LONDON (SOUTH)
Kate Heron, Mark Lawson, Simon Henley

LONDON (NORTH)
Jonathan Speirs, Victoria Thornton, Andy Barnett

LONDON (EAST)
Roger Stephenson, Doreen Lawrence, John Dyer-Grimes

EUROPE
ARCHITECTS Glenn Howells, Niall McLaughlin, Ian Standing,
David Page, Eric Parry, Jeremy Till
LAY ASSESSORS Tony Chapman, Paul Finch, Giles Worsley

RIBA PRIZE WINNERS

STIRLING PRIZE

1996	Hodder Associates	University of Salford
1997	Michael Wilford & Partners	Music School, Stuttgart
1998	Foster & Partners	American Air Museum, Duxford
1999	Future Systems	NatWest Media Centre, Lord's, London
2000	Alsop & Störmer	Peckham Library & Media Centre
2001	Wilkinson Eyre Architects	Magna, Rotherham
2002	Wilkinson Eyre Architects	Millennium Bridge Gateshead

RIBA CLIENT OF THE YEAR

1998	Roland Paoletti
1999	The MCC
2000	The Foreign & Commonwealth Office
2001	Molendinar Park Housing Association, Glasgow
2002	Urban Splash

THE STEPHEN LAWRENCE PRIZE

1998	Ian Ritchie Architects	Terrasson Cultural Greenhouse, France
1999	Munkenbeck + Marshall	Sculpture Gallery, Roche Court
2000	Softroom Architects	Kielder Belvedere
2001	Richard Rose-Casemore	Hatherley Studio, Winchester
2002	Cottrell + Vermeulen	Cardboard Building, Westborough School, Westcliff-on-Sea

THE CROWN ESTATE CONSERVATION AWARD

1998	Peter Inskip & Peter Jenkins	Temple of Concord & Victory, Stowe
1999	Foster & Partners	The Reichstag, Germany
2000	Foster & Partners	JC Decaux UK Headquarters, London
2001	Rick Mather Architects	The Dulwich Picture Gallery
2002	Richard Murphy Architects	Stirling Tolbooth

THE RIBA JOURNAL SUSTAINABILITY AWARD

2000	Chetwood Associates	Sainsbury's, Greenwich
2001	Michael Hopkins & Partners	Jubilee Campus, Nottingham University
2002	Cottrell & Vermeulen	Cardboard Building, Westborough School, Westcliff-on-Sea

THE ADAPT TRUST ACCESS AWARD

2001	Avery Associates Architects	Royal Academy of Dramatic Arts
2002	Malcolm Fraser Architects	Dance Base, Edinburgh

THE ARCHITECTS' JOURNAL FIRST BUILDING AWARD IN ASSOCIATION WITH ROBIN ELLIS DESIGN AND CONSTRUCTION

2001	Walker Architecture	Cedar House, Logiealmond
2002	Sutherland Hussey	Barnhouse, Highgate

SPONSORS

 The RIBA is grateful to all the sponsors who make the awards possible, in particular *The Architects' Journal*, published by EMAP, the main sponsors, who provide the money for the RIBA Stirling Prize and its judging costs. *The Architects' Journal* has been promoting good architecture since 1895. Its weekly news coverage, comprehensive building studies, in-depth technical and practice features and incisive commentary make it the UK's leading architectural magazine, whose authoritative voice has informed generations of architects.

The Architects' Journal also sponsors The Architects' Journal First Building Award in association with Robin Ellis Design and Construction. The prize is intended to mark the successful transition by a young practice from interiors and small works to a complete piece of architecture.

The RIBA would also like to thank:
The ADAPT Trust, sponsors of The ADAPT Trust Access Award. The ADAPT Trust advises on the provision of access for people of all abilities to new and adapted arts and heritage buildings;
The RIBA Journal, which has sponsored The RIBA Journal Sustainability Award since 2000. *The RIBA Journal*, part of CMPI, has been voted by RIBA members one of the most important benefits of membership;
Arts Council England has sponsored The RIBA Client of the Year from its inception in 1998, the prize taking the form of a commissioned work of art by a British artist to be displayed in one of the client's buildings;
The Stephen Lawrence Prize was established in 1998 in memory of the murdered black teenager who aspired to be an architect. It is sponsored by The Goldschmied Foundation, established by RIBA Past President Marco Goldschmied. His foundation also supports the Stephen Lawrence Charitable Trust and in particular its bursary programme, which helps train black architects. www.stephenlawrence.org.uk;
The Crown Estate, sponsor of The Crown Estate Conservation Award first presented in 1998, manages a large and uniquely diverse portfolio of land and buildings across the UK. One of its primary concerns is to make historic buildings suitable for today's users.

All RIBA award winners receive a lead plaque, produced and donated by the Lead Sheet Association, to be placed on the building. The LSA is the primary independent body involved in the promotion and development of the use of rolled lead sheet. The LSA offers authoritative technical advice and comprehensive training services to ensure that rolled lead sheet maintains its matchless reputation as

one of the most established long-lasting and environmentally friendly construction materials. The LSA is proud to have been associated with the RIBA Awards since 1989.

The RIBA would also like to thank the sponsors of the RIBA Stirling Prize Presentation Dinner:
The American Hardwood Export Council, the leading international trade association for the US hardwood industry, who provide technical information on sources of supply, renewal and sustainability of American hardwoods;
BST Global and its UK business partner Eagle Technology, who have 70,000 worldwide users of their business-systems solution, which is specifically designed for the architecture and engineering industries;
Lloyds TSB, sponsors of the firework display, and whose new Bristol headquarters were a catalyst for regeneration of the waterfront and who continue to support the @ Bristol project, venue for the 2003 RIBA Stirling Prize presentation;
Montagu Evans, one of the largest and most effective planning and development consultancies in the country, having achieved planning consent for the Minerva Building, Heron Tower, Swiss Re Tower, City Hall and Palestra;
SIV Architectural Career Management, which is exclusively dedicated to providing effective architectural staff, buildings teams, satisfying clients and ultimately producing more prize-winning buildings;
and Union, the world leader in lock manufacture, committed to applying innovative design approaches with architectural appeal, resulting in aesthetically pleasing, stylish products without compromising on durability or security.

Once again this book, *Architecture 03*, is sponsored by Service Point. Service Point exists to advance document production and management processes.

The RIBA would like to thank Channel 4 for their continuing coverage of The RIBA Stirling Prize in association with *The Architects' Journal*.

PHOTOGRAPHS The RIBA would like to thank all the photographers whose work is published in this book, and who are credited in the main text, for agreeing to waive copyright fees for reproduction by the RIBA of their work in connection with the promotion of the RIBA Awards.

   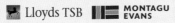

SERVICE POINT > ENTERPRISE DOCUMENT MANAGEMENT SERVICES

Service Point, the world's leading provider of Digital Reprographics, Document Management and Facilities Management to the Architecture, Engineering and Construction industries (A/E/C), takes great pleasure in printing and presenting this edition, as we have done since its inception, of the RIBA Awards book.

Service Point continues to advance the document production and process management surrounding the built environment connecting people, technology and business.

CORE SERVICES >

Plan print from hardcopy or any digital format

Plotting from any digital format

Scan to print > Scan to file > Scan to archive

Large format colour print

Large format scanning up to A0

Volume black & white and colour

Online digital ordering & print

Autovectorisation

Mounting & Heatsealing

Lamination & Encapsulation

Folding & Finishing

INNOVATION SERVICES >

E-Distribution & Print

Online Plan Rooms

Intelligent Archiving Services (IAS)

Electronic Document Management (EDMS)

Project Collaboration

SmartPlot 'Cost Management' software

Supply chain management

Data logistics

CAD software supply & upgrade

'On-site' Rugged computers & Web cams

Process Management consultancy

www.servicepoint.net
0800 634 24 24

Digital Reprographics
Document Management
Facilities Management

SERVICE POINT > SUPPORT THE ENTIRE PROJECT LIFECYCLE

SERVICE POINT DIGITAL REPROGRAPHICS >

As a fully operational bureau and total service provider, Service Point are always on hand to advise you on the technical aspects surrounding your work such as correct file set-up ensuring you always obtain the highest quality finished product. The development of our web technology for the online procurement of digital reprographic services and specialist design office products provides reduced delivery times, online print-on-demand, print and distribution at the point of need as well as job tracking of your orders and projects.

SERVICE POINT DOCUMENT MANAGEMENT >

Service Point offer unique client-based server systems and web-based systems in addition to providing independent advice and consultancy on a number of other solution providers. Our systems assist cost reductions across administration, document production and logistics. They reduce risk of out of revision drawings by creating transparent audit trails. They reduce time through fewer meetings and compressed review processes in the development and management of your multiple construction projects.

SERVICE POINT FACILITIES MANAGEMENT >

Outsourcing can relieve your organisation of the many constraints attendant on research, purchasing and maintaining non-core activities. We believe as the best partner we can deliver your required level of sophistication with the benefits of: > No capital expenditure (CAPEX) > Reduced administrative costs > Accountability by cost centre & project > Improved service levels & quality > Headcount outsourced > Process-driven management. Whatever the need Service Point are Local > Global > Total.

www.servicepoint.net
0800 634 24 24

Digital Reprographics
Document Management
Facilities Management

Service Point